For the Earth
Captain Paul Watson

EARTHFORCE!

AN EARTH WARRIOR'S GUIDE TO STRATEGY

CAPTAIN PAUL WATSON

CHACO PRESS
LOS ANGELES

This is a Chaco Press publication
5218 Donna Maria Lane
La Cañada, California 91011

Typesetting and design by Graphic Touch, San Pedro, CA
Cover Art: Reproduced by Special Permission of Playboy *magazine. ©by* Playboy. *Sculpture by Parviz Sadighian.*

Library of Congress Cataloging-in-Publication Data
92-085357

Earthforce! An earth warrior's guide to strategy.

Environmentalism—Strategy—Watson, Paul; author.

ISBN 0-9616019-5-7

CONTENTS

Foreword by Dave Foreman   v

Acknowledgements   vii

Introduction   1

Principal Contributors   4

Foundation   11

Earthforce!—The Spiritual Foundation
      of an Earth Warrior   22

The Continuum   26

Media Laws   36

The Laws of Ecology   37

The Laws of Eco-Guerrilla Activity   38

    Chapter One: Preparations   39

    Chapter Two: Confrontation   52

    Chapter Three: The Art of Fighting Without Fighting   56

    Chapter Four: Tactics   60

    Chapter Five: Earthforce   63

    Chapter Six: Stealth and Unpredictability   68

    Chapter Seven: Maneuvering   71

    Chapter Eight: Maintaining the Center   74

    Chapter Nine: Field Confrontation   76

    Chapter Ten: Terrain And Situation   78

    Chapter Eleven: The Nine Situations   82

    Chapter Twelve: Attacking With Fire   94

    Chapter Thirteen: The Use of Intelligence Agents   97

The 36 Strategies   103

After Words   111

Bibliography   114

Index   116

Suggestions   118

FOREWORD

By Dave Foreman

I recently received a telephone call from a producer at National Public Radio. She was interviewing a number of people for a new syndicated series about heroes. She wanted to know who my hero was.

I'm fortunate to have many heroes—all of the people who labor to protect the wonderful, buzzing, blossoming abundance and diversity of this blue-green living Earth. These heroes of mine range from middleclass Americans to Kayapo Indians in the Amazon; they include women and men, young and old.

But I didn't require a moment's thought to select my top-of-the-heap hero. There is one person who is in a class of his own in my pantheon of heroes. He is Captain Paul Watson of the Sea Shepherd Conservation Society and skipper of the good ship *Edward Abbey*.

Although I titled my book *Confessions of an Eco-Warrior,* Paul Watson is the greatest Eco-Warrior of all. Operating largely on their own dedication, Paul and his crews enforce international treaties and agreements on the high seas to protect marine mammals and ocean birds from criminal destruction by industrial fishing. Last summer, Watson tore up and confiscated miles of drift nets—floating curtains of death—in the North Pacific and drove illegal Japanese factory fishing ships from the area. Next summer, Watson will be sailing to protect the great whales from illegal slaughter planned by the pirate whaling nations—of Japan, Iceland, Norway, and Denmark.

In all of Watson's voyages and in his land campaigns, no person has ever been harmed or injured.

Captain Watson is called to act because many species of whales, marine mammals, and sea birds face extinction if these outlaw fishers and whalers continue. No nation—not even the United Nations—will enforce the international treaties these criminals violate. Because of this, Watson and his ships have become the international policeman of the sea.

My hero, however, is not just an audacious field commander. Paul Watson has perhaps thought more deeply about strategy than has any other conservationist. His unparalleled strategic sense comes from his study of great military strategists of the past and from his inherent strategic brilliance. All activists defending the wild diversity of life throughout the Earth are fortunate that Captain Watson has written this modern-day primer on strategy. I know no activist—Sierra Club volunteer, Wilderness Society lobbyist, NRDC attorney, conservation biologist, Earth First! blockader, or lone monkeywrencher—who will not profit mightily from reading and studying this book. I believe that I am no slouch at strategy, but I learned much from reading it. I will read again and learn even more.

I know no one who shows greater courage, dedication, and self-confidence in defense of our planet and all of its life. One thousand years from now, sagas will be sung about Captain Paul Watson, defender of the oceans, and people will praise his name because there will still be whales, walruses, dolphins, and sea birds. Paul Watson is the hero of our time. And he is the strategic genius of non-violent ecological defense.

—Dave Foreman
Arroyo Zapata, Sonoran Desert

Dave Foreman is the author of Eco Defense, the Field Guide to Monkey-wrenching *and* Confessions of an Eco-Warrior. *He is a co-founder of the Earth First! movement and is the Executive Editor of* Wild Earth, *the quarterly publication of the Cenozoic Society.*

ACKNOWLEDGEMENTS

I am grateful first and foremost for the inspiration given to me by my Mother Earth and all of her children. With respect, I would like to acknowledge my totem animal—the Grey Wolf.

I would also like to acknowledge the lessons taught to me by Beaver, Orca, Cachalot, Harp Seal, Elephant, Caribou, Bison, Redwood, Eagle, Raven, Grouse, Lilac, and Bear. Also by Wind, River, Lake, Ocean, Mountain, and Spring.

I must acknowledge the profound lessons taught to me by the following peoples: the Oglala Lakota people; the Haida, Kwakuitl, Cree, Kayapo, Gitksan Wet'suwet'en, Beaver, Dene, and Hawaiian peoples; the Masai.

A few human beings whom I have known have been of significant inspiration. These people include Edward Abbey, Cleveland Amory, Father Thomas Berry, Susan Bloom, Sten & Sarah Borg, David Brower, Peter Brown, Captain John Cormack, Aida Flemming, David Foreman, Dian Fossey, Marc Gaede, David Garrick, Jet Johnson, Bob & Bobbi Hunter, Megan Marining, Vicki Miller, Clare & Farley Mowat, Pridim & Annie Singh, David & Tara Suzuki, Rosemary Waldron, and Sharon Whalen.

Thank you to Lavinia Currier for Puu O Hoku as a refuge to gather my thoughts.

A special word of appreciation to my daughter, Lilliolani, for connecting me with the future.

A special thank you to my editor and friend, Marnie Gaede.

A very special thank you to my life mate and partner. Lisa Distefano is both my foundation for inspiration and my anchor in times of stormy weather.

Thank you.

"No one will believe you."

"That is exactly as it is meant to be."

Salavi laughed.

*"But tell them anyway. Tell them once.
Then tell them they have been told and leave."*

—The Vision of Salavi,
*Chichimeca story from
ancient Mexico.*

INTRODUCTION

The Environmental Movement is growing stronger. More and more people are being recruited into the Earthforce each day. Individuals are being recruited because their lives and the habitat around them are being seriously impacted by activity which harms their own health. Becoming an environmentalist is in reality—a question of self preservation.

The fight to save the Earth and ourselves has never been stronger. Some people are ready to stand up for what they stand upon—the Earth beneath their feet. A few are ready to fight. Some are ready to risk their freedom, their health, and their lives for this struggle. There have been some who have already made the sacrifice. Environmental warriors have been jailed, beaten, and murdered. This movement has declared its birthright with the blood of its martyrs.

The movement to protect the Earth has its heroes and heroines. The cause is just enough, and the objectives are many. There is indeed something worth fighting for. Spiritually, the protection of the Earth is the most moral and just cause ever taken up in the history of the human species. The soldier who enlists with the forces of ecological justice joins the ranks of the most noble of warriors.

Within the growing movement for environmental awareness, there is emerging a new force. This force is a Warrior Society of committed, dedicated, and courageous men and women, willing to take the risks needed to serve and protect our Mother—the Earth.

Unfortunately, it is a fractured, confused movement without direction, solid leadership, or tested tactics. Most importantly it is a movement without a strong, powerful, comprehensive strategy.

Who are we?

What do we want?

1

When do we fight?

Where are we going?

How are we going to get there?

Our movement has many questions and few answers.

It is my intention with this book to present guidelines which may help in answering some of these questions.

This is a book on strategy.

Strategy is by nature a martial discipline. In preparing this book I have drawn on four sources.

The first is a small book written twenty-five hundred years ago in China by a general named Sun Tzu. The book, entitled *The Art of War* is considered one of the best works on martial strategy ever written. It has had significant impact on political and military events throughout history. I have applied Sun Tzu's basic principles to the development in this book of a strategy for the ecological warrior.

The second source is another small book written in 1648 in Japan, by a warrior/philosopher named Miyamoto Musashi. The book is entitled *The Book of Five Rings*. Musashi adds to the importance of Sun Tzu's work by providing guidance directly to individuals within a movement.

The third source is the written and presented works of Marshall McLuhan, the Canadian philosopher of media. In our present culture, it is the mass media which determine the boundaries of what we perceive as reality. It is within the media-defined culture that the environmental movement can do battle. An understanding of these media, which dominate global culture, is imperative for the implementation of an effective strategy.

The fourth source, humble in comparison to the first three, is my own experiences as an environmental activist and campaign leader for the past thirty years.

I have attempted to apply in the field, the lessons provided by the other three. I have had failures only where I neglected to adhere to strategy guided by the principles of these three teachers.

I sincerely hope that this book soon may serve to motivate others to expand on strategic ideas for making the environmental movement stronger, more active, more directed, and much more effective.

PRINCIPAL CONTRIBUTORS

Sun Tzu
A wood-carved portrait of Sun Tzu from a thousand-year-old book. Artist unknown.

Miyamoto Musashi
Painting by the Japanese artist Kuniyoshi, c. 1848.

Marshall McLuhan
Photograph by Corinne McLuhan.

Paul Watson
Portrait by Sam Morse-Brown, official artist for the British War Museum. This portrait was done on board the Sea Shepherd II in Bermuda in 1979.

3

PRINCIPAL CONTRIBUTORS

SUN TZU

In China *The Art of War* has been known for centuries as The Thirteen Chapters. The author credited with writing this work is known as Sun Tzu or Sun Wu. Very little is known about him, and even if he existed is in question.

An analysis of the weaponry and political situations described in the book does narrow the period of the authorship to a general time frame. Since the use of crossbows is mentioned, the book was probably written after 400 B.C., which is approximately when the crossbow was introduced into China. The fact that the book mentions large armies and the use of infantry but says not a word about cavalry suggests that the book was written before 320 B.C., which is the time King Wu Ling of Chao State introduced mounted troops.

The question of ancient literary authorship is always open to dispute by academicians. The controversy over the facts about the existence of Sun Tzu has been raging and smoldering for centuries and likely will continue for centuries more.

What is certain is that *The Art of War* was written by a unique and imaginative individual who was well versed in the practical experience of field warfare and conflict.

The text suggests an officer of high rank with exceptional skill in marshaling large numbers of forces in confrontation with formidable opposition.

The man, whatever his real name, was a gifted leader and one of the greatest of generals.

In 1782 *The Art of War* was translated into French by Father Amiot, a Jesuit. The Jesuits introduced the book to Napoleon Bonaparte. There are many historians who believe that The Thirteen Chapters was the secret to the success of the famed French soldier. We know that Napolean utilized mobility, a technique stressed by Sun Tzu.

A careful study of Napolean's campaigns reveals that Sun Tzu's tactics were brilliantly employed by Le Grand Emperor. It is likely that in the end he ignored The Thirteen Chapters in favor of a belief in his own invincibility.

The Vietnam War is a textbook example of what not to do according to the teachings of *The Art of War*. That war was protracted and the supply lines were too long. The United States failed to understand the strategy of the Viet Cong (VC) and the North Vietnamese Army (NVA). General Giap of the NVA read Sun Tzu thoroughly. The West Point officers who opposed him did not include The Thirteen Chapters in their curriculum. The outcome of the war in Indo-China was predicted in advance by students of Sun Tzu.

The United States is a country that wins with weight, like a sumo wrestler sitting on a dwarf. This approach has worked against countries like Panama, Grenada, and Iraq. It is a limited strategy. U.S. foreign policy makes little attempt to employ stratagems for peace. The nation reacts to outside stimuli not unlike an amoeba reacts to light.

The strategy of the United States government fails to recognize the ultimate objective of Sun Tzu's philosophy of strategy.

THE OBJECTIVE OF STRATEGY IS PEACE.

The United States did not and will not defeat communism. Communism defeated itself, just as that other anti-nature economic system called capitalism will eventually do to itself. Both economic systems have little regard for long term objectives and consequences.

For the environmental movement to triumph over the enemies of the Earth, it will be imperative to develop and implement an effective overall approach which contains numerous supporting strategies.

What cannot be achieved with wealth needs to be achieved by stealth. What cannot be achieved by stealth needs to be achieved by profile and media, by the strength and loyalty within the movement, by courage and leadership, and finally by the moral superiority of the cause.

Sun Tzu was a man of war. The environmental movement is essentially tantamount to ecological peace and harmony.

Sun Tzu wrote, " ...the true object of war is peace."
For the ecological warrior the objective is ecological peace.
The path to that peace lies in strategy.

MIYAMOTO MUSASHI

The British have their most legendary historical figure in the personality
of Robin Hood: independent, antiauthoritarian, courageous, ingenious, pos-
sessor of a strong moral code, and the personification of a self-disciplined
independent warrior.

The Japanese have all of these traits and more in the person of Miyamoto
Musashi, who was a man of history, shrouded in the mantle of glorious
legends, all of which have a foundation in actual fact.

Miyamoto Musashi was born in about the year 1584 and is believed to have
died in 1645. He was a master swordsman, probably the greatest master of
kendo in all of Japanese martial history, and he developed the method of
fighting with two swords. He was a rigid adherent to strict self-discipline as
the key to martial arts.

As a youth, Musashi fought on the losing side in the famous battle of
Sekigahara. After that he lived the life of a ronin or masterless samurai, which
gave him both the freedom and the time to devote himself to the mastery of
the art of the sword. He clashed with and defeated the masters of the Yoshioka
school of swordsmanship in Kyoto and the monks of the Hozoin in Nara. His
most famous duel was his triumph over the swordmaster Sasaki Kojiro. He
fought on the losing side at the siege of Osaka castle in 1614 and participated
in the 1637-38 annihilation of Christian forces at Shimabara on the western
island of Kyushu, an event which resulted in the banishment of Christianity
as a religion from Japan for the next two centuries.

In 1640, he became a retainer of the Hosokawa lords of Kumamoto. He was
a skilled painter, poet, and sculptor as well as a swordsman.

Miyamoto Musashi left us with his legacy in the book entitled *Gorin No Sho*
which translates as *The Book of Five Rings* .

Unlike *The Art of* War, which is a book of general strategy, the *Gorin No*

Sho is a book of strategy aimed at the individual.

The author was a man who had transformed himself from a purely instinctive fighter into a warrior who pursued the goals of rigid self-discipline. He developed complete mastery over himself which was accompanied by a sense of oneness with nature. Through Musashi, martial skills, spiritual self-discipline, and aesthetic sensitivity were merged into a single harmonious whole.

Musashi offers guidance for the individual warrior within the Earthforce.

MARSHALL McLUHAN

Herbert Marshall McLuhan was born July 21, 1911 in Edmonton, Alberta.

Professor McLuhan taught at the University of Toronto, from 1946 until his death on December 31, 1980, as a professor of Literature and director of the University's Centre for Culture and Technology.

Marshall McLuhan's perceptions of the media have been documented in his books beginning with *The Mechanical Bride: Folklore of Industrial Man,* which was published in *1951.*

His second book, published in 1964, *was The Gutenberg Galaxy: The Making of Typographic Man* followed by *Understanding Media: The Extensions of Man* in 1964 and *The Medium is the Massage: An Inventory of Effects* in 1967.

McLuhanism is the name given to the media philosophy developed by Marshall McLuhan. The utilization of McLuhan's philosophy in dealing with the media is called a McLuhanesque approach.

Briefly and simply, McLuhan's understanding of the media is thus: the medium is the message. Each medium encourages some approaches to communication and discourages others, regardless of the subject. The media defines culture, and thus defines reality as it is perceived by human populations.

A McLuhanesque approach to the media is to understand what the media wants and then deliver your message to the selected media. If your media is television then you must exploit images and talk in sound bites. If your media is newspapers, then you give more attention to fact as well as attempt to influence the headline.

McLuhan describes various media as "hot" or "cool". Television is a "cool" medium because of its relatively "low definition" which engages its audience in an active way. Print is a "hot" medium, in that its "high definition" encourages detachment. For instance, a war being a hot issue is perceived emotionally on a "cool" media like television but can be read with detachment from a "hot" medium like a newspaper.

The media is an extension of the body. Newspapers and books are extensions of the eye. Electronic media, however, are an extension of the entire nervous system. Newspapers inform. Television entertains and enthrals.

To be successful, the Earth Warrior must be in control of the forces that define the dominant culture. Because the media defines culture, an understanding of media philosophy is essential.

PAUL FRANKLIN WATSON

During the month of March, 1973, I served as a medic with the American Indian Movement and participated in the defense of Wounded Knee. We held out against the superior forces of the United States government for more than two months. It was there that I experienced my first vision in a sweat lodge under the direction of Wallace Black Elk. It was that vision which gave me my Lakota name. It is Grey Wolf Clear Water.

I was born on December 2, 1950 in the hereditary lands of the Huron on the north shore of Lake Ontario. I was raised in the east in the lands of the Alquonquin Micmac on the shores of the Passamaquoddy Bay. For the last twenty years, I have made my home in the traditional lands of the West Coast Salish peoples. I remain linked in spirit to those I fought with at Wounded Knee in the lands of the Lakota.

I was fortunate in having the opportunity to run off to sea at an early age. This gave me first hand experience with numerous cultures. I travelled extensively throughout East and Southern Africa, the Middle East, Europe, and Asia. My sea experience came from service with Norwegian and Swedish merchant vessels, the Canadian Coast Guard, and Mediterranean yachts.

Later, I attended Simon Fraser University in British Columbia to study archaeology, linguistics, and communications.

In 1970, I sailed with the Don't Make a Wave Committee to protest nuclear testing by the United States Atomic Energy Commission on the island of Amchitka in the Alaskan Aleutians. In 1972 we officially changed the name of the Don't Make a Wave Committee, and I became a co-founder of the Greenpeace Foundation.

I left Greenpeace in 1977 and founded the Sea Shepherd Conservation Society.

Since 1977, I have headed the Sea Shepherd Society and continue to do so. In that time, I have led three seagoing expeditions to oppose the Canadian seal slaughter, four sea-going campaigns to protect whales, two high seas expeditions to protect dolphins, five expeditions to oppose drift-netters, and one land based expedition to protect wolves in British Columbia and the Yukon.

During this time I was responsible for or oversaw the sinking of eight illegal whaling ships, the sinking of one sealing ship, the blockading of a Canadian sealing fleet, the destruction of a whale processing plant, the paint bombing of a Soviet trawler, the ramming of two Japanese drift net vessels, the ramming of a Mexican tuna seiner, the ramming of a Taiwanese drift netter, the shutting down of a Japanese dolphin hunt, the closing down of seal hunts in Great Britain and Ireland, the landing in Soviet Siberia to document illegal whaling activities, and the interference in killing operations against marine mammals in thirteen countries. I was also responsible for inventing the tactic of tree-spiking to protect old growth forests.

Most importantly, these things were accomplished without causing or sustaining a single injury to our opposition or to my crew. Additionally these missions did not result in a single criminal or civil conviction against myself, my society, or my crew.

Even more importantly, these missions resulted in the salvation of the lives of tens of thousands of whales, hundreds of thousands of dolphins, and millions of seals, not to mention hundreds of wolves and hundreds of thousands of trees.

I mention the above accomplishments as proof of my credibility in addressing the issue of strategy.

Therefore, armed with the penned ingenuity of Sun Tzu, the
self-discipline of Musashi, the perceptions of media and
culture by McLuhan, I can now incorporate my own
personal experience formulating this book.
With the heartfelt and sincere wish
that I may make a contribution
in a small way—towards
directing your travel
along the path of
a Warrior for
and of the
Earth.

FOUNDATION

Strategy is to be found through five paths. These paths are named after the natural spirits of Earth, Water, Fire, Wind, and the Vision Quest.

The Earth is the foundation. It is difficult to realize strategy through a single discipline. Know the smallest things and the biggest things, the shallowed things and the deepest things. Always keep an open mind and realize that no answers are final nor firm. This is the first step to realizing the path of the five ways.

The second way is Water. With water as the basis, the spirit becomes like water. Water adopts the shape of its receptacle, it is sometimes a rivulet and sometimes a wild sea. Water is clarity. Water is purity. The spirit of victory is the same be the victory small or great. The strategist makes small things into big things. In principal of strategy, the water path is to have one thing and to know many things.

The third way is Fire. This is the path that deals with fighting. Fire is fierce regardless of the size of the flame. The spirit can become big or small. What is big is easy to perceive. What is small is difficult to perceive. It is difficult for large numbers of people to change position, so their movements are easy to predict. An individual that can easily change movements is difficult to predict. The essence of Fire is that you must train day and night if you are to make decisions without hesitation. In strategy it is necessary to regard training as a normal routine of your life without changing your spirit. This is the path of combat and confrontation.

The fourth way is the way of the Wind. This is the understanding of the lessons of the past and of all cultures. It is difficult to know yourself if you do not know others. To all roads there are side paths. You cannot study one way and allow your spirit to diverge. If you are following one way and allow yourself to diverge a little, this will later become a large divergence.

The fifth and last path is the road into the Vision world. The Vision quest is that which has no beginning and no end. Attainment of this principle means to not attain this principle. The way of strategy is the way of nature. When you begin to understand the power of nature, knowing the rhythm of all situations, you will begin to be able to act naturally and to fight naturally.

In summation:

The Earth is your foundation. Seek to be aware of all things. Keep an open mind and understand that you cannot and you will not ever perceive the truth that is reality. There are many realities. Hold on to your own reality and evolve from it. Do not dismiss the reality of others.

Bend like the willow. Flow like water. Be clear, be pure, and cherish your achievements. Build upon your strengths and be creative. Be focused, but do not lose sight of what is around you.

In conflict, you must be fierce. Learn to calculate. Cultivate the skill of Seeing. You must appreciate discipline. You must be prepared.

You must be aware of the past. The study of history is imperative. You must be aware of what is happening in the world of the present - all things in general. However, never lose your focus.

You must be in tune with the natural rhythms of the Earth. You must surrender reason to intuition. You must not fear death.

THE STRATEGIC ARTS

Strategy is the craft of the Earth Warrior.

There are few Earth Warriors in the world today who really understand the Way of Strategy.

There are various strategic arts. There is:

> The strategy of the Healer.
> The strategy of the Communicator.
> The strategy of the Artist.
> The strategy of the Infiltrator.
> The strategy of the Catalyst.
> The strategy of the Shaman.

A human must choose a strategy based on intuitive inclination.

The strategy of the Healer is to restore. This may mean restoration of an eco-system or the practice of natural healing arts as applied to living organisms. The healer seeks to restore, to rejuvenate, to refresh, and to repair. For the human practitioner, the objective is to counter the negative consequences of human action with restorative actions. This way requires a gentle nature, a caring nature, and the ability to absorb the negative from without while preserving the positive within.

The strategy of the Communicator is to communicate ideas and to teach the Way of all Earth Warriors. This strategy requires a curious nature, the skill of writing, and the ability to speak and to be understood.

The strategy of the Artist is to demonstrate respect for the Earth, to bridge the ever widening gap between natural humanity and alienated humanity, and to connect the present with the past and the future. This strategy requires intuition, imagination, and a natural ability to communicate effectively.

The strategy of the Infiltrator is to affect change from within the fortifications of enemies of the Earth. This strategy requires the skills of espionage, creative sabotage, and proficiency in the skills valued by the forces of anthropocentrism. This Way requires strong determination and dedication.

The Way of the Catalyst is to confront and to provoke. The followers of this art are like acupuncture needles stimulating a response. Those who follow this Way are also like lightning bolts, striking quickly and with consequence. This strategy requires great courage, stubbornness, determination, ambition, leadership skills, and complete dedication to the Way of the Earth Warrior.

The strategy of the Shaman is to connect the spiritual reality to the material reality. The Shaman is a spiritual guide for all Earth Warriors. The Way of the Shaman requires the skills of intuition, the ability to tap the vision world, and the skills of perception and empathy. The Shaman must be selfless and dedicated completely to the power of the Earthforce.

Whatever strategy is chosen, it must be remembered that the Way of the Earth Warrior requires an absolute acceptance that the Earth is life eternal and individuals must die. The fear of personal death must be overcome in order for an individual to progress as a Warrior serving the Earth.

The Earth Warrior must overcome all concerns of personal welfare and personal ambition. To think only of the practical benefit of knowing the Way is to lose the Way.

When your thinking rises above the concern for your own welfare, wisdom which is independent of thought appears. Whoever thinks deeply on things, even though with careful consideration of the future, will usually think around the basis of personal welfare. The result of such thinking will bring about negative results for the Earth. It is very difficult for most people to rise above thinking of their own welfare.

So when you embark upon something, before you begin, you must fix your intention on the Four Oaths and put selfishness behind you. Then you will not fail.

THE FOUR OATHS

1. Never lose respect for the Way of the Earth Warrior.
2. Be of service to the Earth and all of her children.
3. Be respectful to the Earth and all of her children.
4. Get beyond love and grief, beyond personal ambition:
   Exist for the good of the Earth and all of her children.

Never be concerned with the idea of success or failure. The Way of the Earth Warrior is to see things through.

Recently there have been people getting on in the world as environmentalists, as conservationists, as defenders of the rights of animals, as healers of the plights of the Earth and the afflictions of people. If we look closely, we see that these people in many cases are motivated by profit or glory. They have corrupted the strategy. Some men and women are using the issues and taking advantage of the rape of the Earth and her children to sell themselves. They are looking for profit or fame. Some are looking to co-opt the cause to further anthropocentric agendas.

Immature strategy is a cause of grief.

THE STRATEGY OF THE HEALER

To follow this strategy it must be understood that the Earth is a living organism, as are all planets, as are all stars. Life is more complicated than we can ever hope to imagine. The diversity of life is infinite relative to the finite ability of the human mind to comprehend. We will never have the capacity to understand all. If there is a power that exists and that does understand all, then it is not within the realm of human attainment to ascertain such things. All attempts to do so will result in conflict and failure.

We must learn to be content with not consciously knowing. This is not difficult once you accept that you are a part of all that there is and that you will always be a part of all that there is. There is no collective death, only continual individual death and renewal. Because you are an integral part of the Earth, knowledge will make itself known to you only when it is necessary that you know and only when your intent is clear. The Earth is the collective sum of her parts. The organic and the inorganic chemistry of her being combine with the immaterial to make her whole. Because of this, all of her parts are important and must be respected.

The strategy of the Healer is an understanding that to heal a piece of the Earth, to heal a human, a tree, an elephant, or a river is a task that is equal in respect. The life of a human is equal to the life of an animal. The life of an animal is equal to the life of a plant. The life of a plant is equal to the state of being of a mountain or a lake.

The definition of alive is a state of being. Water is life. Rocks are living. Life can be defined as IS, the state of being. If an Earth Warrior decides to apply the strategy of the Healer, this must be understood. The strategy is the same but the skills and tactics vary.

To heal a human being, the Healer must be knowledgeable of anatomy, of the properties of herbs, the benefits of nutrition, the needs of the body, mind, and spirit. The Healer of humans must know how to set broken bones, to abate a fever, and to direct energies towards helping the body to heal itself. These people may study naturopathic or homeopathic skills or the art of shiatsu or other hands-on skills. They may teach and direct in the fields of physical education, nutrition, psychology, or meditation.

There are many healing skills. The choice is open, the strategy remains the same.

The same strategy applies to the healer of nonhuman animals and differs naught. The skills and knowledge will differ. The anatomy of non-human animals must be studied. An intuitive understanding of the nature of nonhumans is a necessity.

The Healer of non-human animals may become a naturopathic veterinarian or an individual that works for the welfare of these beings. Animal welfare workers may choose to work with domestic or wild animals. Conservationists will seek to protect the rights and habitat of wild animals and protect them from the onslaught of the baser human animals. The application of the art of healing animals by humans must be for the welfare and well-being of the animal and not for the purpose of human utilitarian needs.

The same strategy applies to the Healer of plants. Again, the skills and knowledge will differ. The workings of plant-life must be understood.

The healer of plants may become a botanist or a gardener. It is important here to remember that for the human healer of plants, the healing must be applied for the good of the plant and not for the purpose of human utilitarian needs.

The same strategy applies to the inorganic. The skills and knowledge will differ. The workings of inorganic chemistry must be understood.

Regardless of the being in need of healing, the Healer must respect the recipient of the healing process. At the same time, the Healer must respect the interdependence of other states of being.

THE STRATEGY OF THE COMMUNICATOR

The art of the Communicator is to teach the nature of the Earth to others. The responsibility for communicating the strategies of the Earth Warrior lie with the Communicator.

If the Communicator takes the path of the teacher, then the primary purpose of teaching is to show the paths of the Earth Warrior. Teach by example. Do not dictate. Teach with respect, both for the art and for the student.

Above all the teacher must be aware of the responsibility inherent in this path.

If the student is a child, it is important that the teacher understand the nature of children. It is important that the child both trusts and respects the teacher. Respect also the intuitiveness of the child. Nurture the natural abilities of children.

If the student is an adult, it is important that the teacher appreciate the dependence of adults. Understand that the adult mind is not as open as the child. Understand the limitations of the adult mind. It is the rare teacher that can overcome the limitations caused by the prior conditioning of adults.

If the path of the journalist is chosen, it is important to recognize that objectivity in media is rare in human cultures. Journalists favor either the right or the left, the biocentric or the anthropocentric. The journalist who sides with the Earth must utilize the media as a tool to promote the best interests of the Earth.

The art of the journalist is important because the media is the key to reaching the hearts and minds of the general population. This discipline works best when coupled with the strategy of the infiltrator. However, the strategy can be applied overtly in the limited media of the movement.

THE STRATEGY OF THE ARTIST

The strategy of the Artist is a difficult discipline to follow. This strategy requires self-discipline both in applying and mastering a natural skill and in resisting temptation from the material world.

When following this way it is important to never forget that the objective of the artist is to serve the Earth, to bridge the ever widening gap between biocentric humanity and humanity alienated from nature.

This strategy requires a powerful intuition and an even more powerful imagination.

The strategy of the Artist has in recent years been preempted by the material world with co-opting and indulgence of the ego. Thus the most important strength to cultivate for the follower of this strategy is humility.

It must be remembered that art is merely a reflection of the natural world, a way of perceiving other realities. It is important that the artist serve the Earth and the future and not just self interest. It is important that the artist serve the Earth and not the pseudo world of art itself.

For many people, art has become a paramount concern. Some people fervently believe that the works of humanity are of utmost importance.

The pyramids, the Old Masters, the symphonies, sculpture, architecture, film, photography, and the things that we have chosen to define our culture or to define ourselves create a belief that in these fleeting material things we will find our identity. All of these things are worthless to the Earth when compared with any one species of bird, or insect, or plant. The creations of the Earth are supreme and the only importance. The creations of humans are vanity.

Selling a Van Gogh painting for sixty million dollars is an obscenity. The artist did not profit by this sale. This particular Japanese buyer raped thousands of square miles of rainforests from all over the world to acquire the wealth to purchase a bit of coloured hydro-carbon splattered on canvas. The artist was debased by the greedy destruction of biological complexity.

The strategy of the Artist must recognize that works are merely reflections on the natural beauty of the Earth and Universe.

People admire, acquire, and possess artworks in the hopeful belief that in these human generated things they may find their center or their identity. Very few do. Only those who actually practice the strategy of the Artist find their center in the act of creating.

It is important that the artist contribute to the welfare of each subject. If a painter specializes in whales and if the work is profitable, then the profit should benefit the whales. If a musician is inspired by the trees or the mountains, then contributions should be given for the protection of trees and mountains.

If the artist follows the path of architecture, it is important that his or her creations do not embarrass or conflict with the Earth.

THE STRATEGY OF THE INFILTRATOR

This is the art of espionage and covert sabotage. The Infiltrator should not have a public record of actions in support of the Earth. This type of Warrior must be able to assimilate culturally with the opposition.

Overtly, a practicing member of an anthropocentric religion, covertly a dedicated follower of the natural spiritual realities.

Overtly, a person who respects the anthropocentric laws, covertly a dedicated follower of the natural laws.

Overtly, a person who respects the anthropocentric system, covertly a person dedicated to opposing the forces of anthropocentrism.

This is a difficult Art. The temptations are great. It can be a lonely position. It is also one of the most effective means of opposing the enemy.

It is wise for the Infiltrator to liaison only with a person who follows the strategy of the Catalyst. It is wiser still to liaison with no other person.

This is a path without recognition or of belated recognition, sometimes posthumous recognition, sometimes with the stigma of being historically cast as an enemy of the Earth. And yet, human perceptions of your contributions to the Earth and the children of the future are not relevant.

The Infiltrator should be well educated within the confines of the established educational system.

The Infiltrator should never give overt gifts to groups following the strategies of the Earth Warrior. This can be traced.

Infiltrators may choose careers in law, in business, in the military, in government, or in the diplomatic service.

Infiltrators can covertly pass on information to concerned groups of individuals.

Other tactics that can be utilized are: the spreading of dis-information, outright sabotage of technical equipment, erasing files to protect people in the Movement, and covert re-direction of funds.

Sometimes an infiltrator may choose to go public if the advantages are worth the cost of exposure. This would mean directing yourself towards the strategy of the Catalyst.

Sometimes an infiltrator may be overtly sympathetic but is beyond direct proof of involvement.

THE STRATEGY OF THE CATALYST

The art of the Catalyst is a demanding discipline. The main objective of this strategy is to act like an acupuncture needle to stimulate actions and change.

This type of Earth Warrior must maintain a high public profile. Experience in manipulating media is important. The individual must be a good speaker, a good writer, and a person of action.

This is a strategy where the Warrior must lead by example.

Charisma is a quality that should be cultivated. The Catalyst must be strong, stubborn, righteous, and maintain a positive attitude.

The Warrior choosing this strategy will lead, establish, and direct organizations.

In the Movement, those who follow the strategy of the Catalyst will be public speakers, media spokespeople, and leaders of actions.

Catalysts must continually expose themselves to danger, to public ridicule, to the equally annoying public adoration, and to harassment by the guardians of established law, the police, and intelligence agencies.

The strategy of the Catalyst is followed by the generals of the Movement. They are the primary strategists for the directions of operations of an overt and direct nature.

THE STRATEGY OF THE SHAMAN

The Art of the Shaman requires rigid self-discipline. The Shaman is the connection between the spiritual interpretation of the forces of nature and those warriors of the other paths who have also chosen to serve the Earth.

The true Shaman does not wear the cloak of a guru. The virtues here are wisdom, intuition, humility, discipline, and sacrifice.

ALL ARE ONE

The Shaman is the Light of strategy. The Healer is the Heart of strategy. The Communicator is the Voice of strategy. The Artist is the soul of strategy. The Infiltrator is the Eyes and Ears of strategy. The Catalyst is the Will of strategy.

Together the disciplines harmonize into a working movement of individual warriors united by a bond of love, respect, and duty to the Earth.

EARTHFORCE!
The Spiritual Foundation of an Earth Warrior

A Warrior's life is an eternal quest for wisdom, harmony, and understanding.

It must, however, be appreciated that complete knowledge, peace, and enlightenment will not be realized. If you do not accept this, then disappointment, despair, and cynicism lie waiting for you in the future.

It is the quest that is real and it is in the quest that near perfection, near harmony and a glimpse of understanding may be found.

For yourself, there is only now - the present. The past belongs to those who came before. The future belongs to the children. Lessons can be drawn from the past. Concern and love for those unborn may guide your actions. But it is only the present that you can bend to your will, only the present that sustains you, and it is only in the present that you can act. The past is for scholars. The future is for dreamers. The present is for the warrior activist. Although it must be said that a true Warrior is a scholar, an activist and a dreamer.

The most important trait for a Warrior to cultivate is self-discipline. In fact it is only self-discipline that separates a Warrior from those that simply exist. You must rise above the masses of humanity and through sacrifice and by the force of your will you can go where no others dare go, you will see what others fear to look upon, you will experience life in the way it is meant to be experienced to it's fullest.

It is not my place to tell any other how to think or what to think. Your quest is your own. Your way must be your way, not mine, and certainly not the way of the collective mass of humanity, the destroyers of nature and the befoulers of the Earth.

I am simply a guide and a humble one at that. I can only direct you towards the path with the benefit of the little knowledge that I have acquired. I cannot walk the path with you nor can any other person. You must walk it alone with courage and with dignity.

But I can tell you that to be successful you must attempt to clean the slate of your soul of all the nonsense that anthropocentric society has stuffed into your head. You must throw off reason and cultivate intuition. You must allow your guidance to come from within and no longer from without.

You must touch the Earth. It is from the Earth that you have sprung and it is from the Earth that you receive your nourishment and your strength. The Earth Warrior serves the Earth. The Earth comes first - always.

The protection, conservation, and preservation of the Earth is the foremost concern of the Earth Warrior. You must be prepared to risk all, including your life and liberty, to uphold the sacred integrity of the Earth.

You can do this only if you truly believe in the sacredness of the Earth, the sanctity of nature, and the holiness of the wilderness.

The major failing within the environmental movement is the failure to see the Earth as sacred.

Anthropocentric culture has taught most of us to look upon anthropocentric beliefs as sacred. Thus it is considered blasphemy to spit upon the Black Stone in Mecca or to dismantle the Wailing Wall in Jerusalem or to desecrate a statue in the Vatican. If any person were to do any of these things, they would be dealt with quickly and violently and anthropocentric society would applaud their murders. Yet when loggers assault the sacredness of the remaining redwood forests of California, when they desecrate the natural cathedrals of the natural world, the environmental movement responds with petitions and letters or protest signs.

If our view of the redwood forests is that they are sacred, then their destruction should be considered by us to be blasphemous, and the destroyers should be quickly and violently dealt with. To many environmentalists, the talk of sacredness in nature is nothing more than rhetoric. The desecration of the sacred, if the sacred is really sacred, will always inspire gut anger and will in all cases provoke an active response.

To the Earth Warrior, a redwood is more sacred than a religious icon, a species of bird or butterfly is of more value than the crown jewels of a nation, and the survival of a species of cacti is more important than the survival of monuments to human conceit like the pyramids.

The natural rage inspired by those who violate or attack the sacred must be channelled by the Earth Warrior through discipline. The enemies of the Earth can only be met with an opposition that wields superior strategy and superior tactics. Numbers and technology can always be defeated with the application of superior strategy and tactics.

In anthropocentric society, a harsh judgement is given to those that destroy or seek to destroy the creations of humanity. Monkey-wrench a bulldozer and they will call you a vandal. Spike a tree and they will call you a terrorist. Liberate a coyote from a trap and they will call you a thief. Yet if a human destroys the wonders of creation, the beauty of the natural world, then anthropocentric society calls such people loggers, miners, developers, engineers and businessmen.

A strong positive spirituality must be cultivated with its roots firmly implanted in a biocentric perspective.

The Earth Warrior is a biocentrist. An Earth Warrior serves the biosphere.

For an Earth Warrior there is no compromise with the anthropocentrist.

The Earth and her children are first.

The interests of the whole is more important than the self interest of one species, any species including our own.

The Earth Warrior is equal to the wolf, the whale, the willow, the wasp, and the wren.

Species are more important than individuals.

Within the context of species equality can be found a sense of planetary belonging. To be a part of the whole is to be free of the alienation caused by an individual species like our own becoming divorced from the biospheric family of life.

To be spiritually liberated from the chains of anthropocentrism, you must ruthlessly abandon all attitudes that place humanity on a special pedestal of worthiness.

Christ, Mohammed, and Bhudda were primates, cousins to the chimpanzee and the mountain gorilla, just as we are all the children of a species of naked simians. In primateness, we can find family.

Although anthropocentric humans may consider themselves to be divine legends in their own mind, the biological reality is that they are simply overly glorified, conceited apes.

God is not a monkey.

God is the unknown, the feminine force in divine harmony with the masculine force, the is and the is not, the positive and the negative, the alpha and the omega. God is anything and everything that can be imagined.

But the one thing God is not - is definable. Attempts by the anthropocentrics to define the unknown, to finite the infinite, have only led and continue to lead to ecological holocaust and the deaths of billions of lives.

In embracing the biocentric foundations of a natural biocentric perspective, you must abandon and dismiss the dictates of anthropocentric theologies.

The truth is not to be found in Christian icons, Judaic writings, Islamic rules, Buddhist meditation, or any of the theological inventions of humankind.

The truth can only be found by realizing that it cannot be found and that all is not knowable, that the infinite can never be comprehended by the finite.

The purpose of life is life itself. The purpose of death is rebirth. The purpose of birth is death. The immortality of humanity as in all species is to be found in the Continuum.

In the ballads of the Frankish knights lie encoded the true essence of the warrior's path. The Grail romances are the foundation of European chivalry. In King Arthur we find the definition of glory and nobility which is great valor in a cause of certain defeat. Arthur's greatness was in serving a cause greater than himself, knowing that he would inevitably fail. In his failure he won for his cause the time needed by those he did serve.

Environmentalists serve the Earth and we fight to buy time and preserve territory, a minute at a time, an inch at a time. Our victory lies in accumulation of effort. To serve the cause effectively lies in the ability to direct passions most strategically over the long period of time.

THE CONTINUUM

"To us the ashes of our ancestors are sacred
and their resting place is hallowed ground."

—Chief Seattle
Chief of the Dwamish

Time flows like blood through the veins of reality. Time is the measure of all things. To all living beings, time dictates a beginning of self-awareness and an end to self-awareness. To exist within the flow of time is to take on the reality of sentience for a brief period before returning to the reality of non-sentience.

Life is energy and energy cannot be created nor destroyed. Life is a transition, a link between the sentience of the past and the sentience of the future.

All living things upon the Earth are a part of the Earth. All living things upon the Earth have always been a part of the Earth. All living things upon the Earth will forever be a part of the Earth. For in truth, all that is alive upon the Earth IS the Earth herself. All is one. We are the Earth and we are indivisible from ourselves. All life is interdependent.

All that came before and all that will come later are also one and the same. Past, present, and future are different stretches of the same river. Like the molecules of water in a river, the living beings of the past remain connected to the living beings of the future through the living beings of the present.

This is the Continuum of life.

At the present time, humanity is divided into two distinct and radically different perspectives. People are anthropocentric or they are biocentric.

Anthropocentric people have chosen to step out of the flow for a brief period. They no longer feel the connection to their ancestors nor do they feel kinship with the children of the future. They do not even feel kinship to the other non-human beings of the present.

I said for a brief period and this is because anthropocentric thought, which is a deviation, will exist only briefly before self-destructing. The Continuum is the guide for navigating the river of life. Without the Continuum, then life has no direction and such a life-style will run counter to the Ecological Laws and thus will create ecological disorder.

The biocentric person naturally takes an interest in the people of the past. Aboriginal people are well aware of the deeds and lives of their forebears, going back hundreds of years. Anthropocentric people give little thought to the deeds and lives of their grandparents or even that of their parents.

Children of all cultures express an interest in those who came before them. The people of the Earth will share their knowledge of their ancestors with their children. The people who have divorced themselves from the Earth will dismiss this knowledge as unimportant.

A knowledge of history, both natural and human, is an essential discipline for the Earth Warrior.

Natural history gives us an understanding of evolution and thus a more humble appreciation of our rightful place as human animals upon this planet. Natural history teaches us the connection between all living beings of the present with all living beings from the past. Natural history is the story of the Continuum of all life on Earth.

The written history of humanity is an anthropocentric history for the most part. There are, however, glimpses of wiser cultures within the written record, although these cultures have usually been recorded only when they have hindered or have been a victim of anthropocentric progress. Records of pre-Columbian people of Turtle Island now called the Americas or pre-European cultures of what is now called Australia present fascinating glimpses of biocentric cultures. The same holds true for early pre-Roman Northern European history or pre-Bantu South African history.

From human recorded history we can learn about biocentric and anthropocentric attitudes and the evolution of the two, the conflict between them and the comparative ecological impact of both.

It is through history and anthropology that we can learn from the mistakes of our ancestors. It is through history that we can resurrect the ecologically more positive life styles of our more enlightened ancestors. It is through history that we can learn the results, both success and failure, of the application of different strategies.

The study of history also expands our knowledge of events past so as to draw us into the reality of the past. This will give us a more solid position within the Continuum of Life. To not have an understanding of history is to be like a person suffering amnesia. Without memory you are not complete. A memory of one's personal life may be sufficient for the anthropocentric individual. The biocentric person, on the other hand, needs the knowledge of the past to be fulfilled. Without this knowledge, the past within the Continuum is foggy and perceptions of the present are distorted.

We can approach our past in the Continuum through a knowledge of history. An understanding of the future can be had by cultivating our natural, intuitive ability to envision.

Vision is a difficult ability to harness if stifled by rational or logical thought. Vision comes from the heart and soul and not from the head. Vision is the ability to see the past, the present, and the future.

Through knowledge and intuition we can see the past. Through intuition and our senses, we can perceive the present. Through intuition and imagination we can envision the future.

Most anthropocentric peoples have little desire to glimpse or even to be curious of the future. The average anthropocentric look into the future concerns the next pay cheque, the next mortgage payment, or the possibility of sending their children to a suitable university. Their idea of the future is self-interested. When they do talk of the more distant future, they usually limit their discussions to how they see the world to come in terms of technological innovation. Talk of space travel, of more efficient timesaving gadgets, or life extension discoveries monopolize most of the discussions. Very little is said about pollution, species extinction, over-population, scarcity of food and water, and on and on. A blind faith in human technological inventiveness allays all concerns in this direction. To the anthropocentric mind, tomorrow will of course be better than today, because they also believe that today is

28

better than yesterday.

This vision and the reality our descendents experience may be radically different.

To the biocentric, the children and people of tomorrow are real people. The children of the world of five hundred years from now are as much our children as those who directly and physically came from contact with our own bodies. The biocentric loves not only the child of his or her loins but also the baby, child, and adult who is birthed by the woman who will be reality by virtue of a direct link between the now and tomorrow.

Those who call themselves environmentalists today work most directly for the welfare and well-being of all those who will live throughout the generations to come. Environmental activists today may be reviled, ridiculed, hated, and condemned by anthropocentric attitudes, but to the people of tomorrow, they will make excellent ancestors.

Environmental activists represent the majority of humans, because we represent all those billions of people who have yet to be born over the next ten thousand plus years. In addition, environmentalists represent the billions of individuals of the tens of millions of fellow citizen species.

Born of the Earth, we return to the Earth. The soil beneath our feet contains the material reality of the ancestors of all species. Without the expended lives of the past, there would be little soil. For this reason, the soil itself is our collective ancestry and thus the soil should be as sacred to humans as it is to our fellow citizen species.

The water of the Earth is the blood of the Earth and within its immensity will be found the molecules of water which once enlivened the cells of our ancestors of all species. The water you drink once coursed through the blood of the dinosaurs, or was drunk by Pre-Cambrian ferns, or was expended in the urine of a mastodon. Water has utilized the lives of all living things as a part of its circulatory system. All life contains water. Therefore water is sacred.

The air that we breathe has passed through countless living respiratory systems and thus has been chemically stabilized by plants and animals. Without the lives that have gone before, there would be no air to breathe. The life of the past has nurtured the atmosphere. Therefore the air is sacred.

Because soil, water, and air are sacred due to the contribution of all past lives, then it must be recognized that the past is sacred, and thus the memories of our ancestors is sacred.

Our lives in the present should be sacred to all the living things of the future.

In the realm of humanity however, the contribution of humans of the present will be as an object lesson on why natural human beings should not stray blindly from the path of nature and outside the flow of the Continuum.

For those in the present, the only way to contemplate the future is through feelings of love. Love for our children and our children's children and their children ad infinitum or to the end of our species and beyond to the end of the Earth.

Our actions and our decisions must always weight the consequences for future peoples. There is an Iroquois expression that states, "make no decision without first taking into account the impact that it will have over the next seven generations."

When you father or mother a child, you are obligated within the Continuum to bear responsibility for the protection, nourishment, nurturing, and education of the child. To not do so is the greatest of irresponsibilities and one of the gravest crimes a human can commit.

With the birth of a child, the parents set in motion a series of events which will ripple forward into the future of the Earth. With the birth of one, you bring forth thousands. The psychology of one generation deeply affects the psychology of the next and so on.

Within the context of nature, all animals abort their young if they cannot guarantee the welfare and health of their off-spring. In some cases, the very fact of an increase in population may jeopardize the health of the child. In such a case, the unborn is sacrificed in order to maintain the stabilization of the natural order.

Abortion is a serious responsibility and it is a responsibility that must be borne by the females of all animal species. Males and females have responsibilities equal in value to the welfare of both. Abortion however is a female responsibility. Only she can decide if she is psychologically and physiologically capable of giving birth and sustaining the development of a child. For this she must also be secure in the support of her male partner. The decision is hers and the emotional burden is also hers to bear and hers to deal with, again hopefully with the support of the responsible male.

As long as the unborn baby is physically connected to the mother, the child and the mother are one and the same. The child is not an individual if it cannot sustain itself. The woman, as mistress of her own body, has every right to judge and decide on the welfare and future of her body, mind, and soul.

When anthropocentric society dictates that the law of the state over-rules the freedom of the individual to decide her own fate and chart her own course, such legislation amounts to the rape of the individual woman by the brutish might of the faceless state.

To force a woman to produce a child against her will is rape.

By outlawing pre-natal abortion, the state brings into being the practise of post-natal abortion and thus a child is set on the road of life burdened with the emotional scars of being unloved, uncared for, and abused.

Deviant criminal behaviour, from sexual crimes to mass murder, can be attributed to the ranks of those who had post-natal abortion inflicted upon them by the dictates of the nation state over the responsible choice of the Mother.

This is not to say that all those who decide to have children are making responsible choices. So alienated from nature have we become that we as a species have been grossly guilty of bringing forth children without the guidance of the Continuum.

As a result, the most dangerous threat to the future has come about: the lethal explosion of human populations.

Anthropocentric society values quantity of life over quality of life. The greater the numbers of humans on the planet, the cheaper each individual life becomes. As a result, anthropocentric society has slaughtered over one hundred million people in the twentieth century alone.

Nation states require population growth, if not through births then through immigration. Numbers mean political strength and bodies to employ in industry, agriculture, and warfare. These are the three great plagues that anthropocentric society has inflicted upon the natural world.

The Catholic church condemns both birth control and abortion because its institutionalized strength lies in the number of worshippers and not in individual devoutness.

In a biocentric world like the one that humans lived in for tens of thousands of years before the invention of agriculture, small groups of humans can live harmoniously with nature. Today, evidence of this harmonious relationship can be seen in the cultures of the bushmen in Africa or some of the native tribes in South America or Indo-China.

Prior to the development of agriculture, the human species stabilized itself with zero population growth. Since the development of agriculture and especially since the development of industry and technology, the Earth has witnessed incredible exponential human population growth. In fact, there are now more human beings alive on the planet in the present than have cumulatively existed in the past.

The only solution to this situation is for the implementation of negative population growth. Since negative population growth must be through choice, the outlook of achieving it within the context of an anthropocentric culture is remote.

But unless the human species makes such a choice to consciously and humanely lower its population, then we must anticipate the interference of nature and the consequences that this will bring.

Our deviant behaviour will be corrected by nature when our populations exceed the carrying capacity of the Earth. This will happen within the next century. The calculations based on present day population growth indicates a population of nearly forty billion by 2100 A.D.

Once our populations exceed carrying capacity, the population will crash due to natural factors like starvation, disease, lack of water, lack of shelter, pollution, and conflict. Prior to the collapse there will be an insidious decline in the quality of life for all living things.

There will be survivors just as there were survivors of the great killer plagues of Europe which began in the twelfth century. However, the experience will not be a pleasant one. The death, the misery, the suffering, and the humiliation of such an experience will make all the trials and tribulations of past human history pale in significance and impact.

And the survivors, unless they return to the Continuum, will set in motion a pattern of life styles which will lead again and again to population crashes.

Such a legacy should not be bestowed upon future people by our lack of vision today. Do we wish to leave our children's children with a heritage of death, misery, and destruction or do we wish to transmit our love through the ages by taking steps to preserve the beauty and diversity of the living Earth as it is today, as it has survived to this day?

Remember, we, the children of today, were robbed by many of those of our ancestors who slaughtered, raped, and pillaged their way through the natural world. There are thousands of animals and plants that did not survive because of the lack of vision expressed in the greed of some of our forebears. Today, the greed of many of us will rob the children of the future of similar treasures.

It was only during the last five hundred years that the great biocentric cultures of Australia and the Americas were destroyed. In that brief time, anthropocentric human civilization has all but destroyed the natural wonders and treasures of the virgin expanses of lands that were dwelling in natural harmony.

What our children's children need from us is the expression of our rage as Warriors. We need to fight, to set an example by our actions. We need to exert with all of our individual and collective strength the will to place ourselves back within the embrace of the bosom of the Earth.

We need to return to the garden of the natural world. We need to revolt against anthropocentric thought. We owe such a revolution to those of the future. Through our revolution we can absolve ourselves of the sins of the past.

We of the present are responsible as a species for the actions of our species in the past. We of the present are responsible as a species for the well-being of those of our species yet to be born. We of the present are also responsible for our actions in the present and the consequences that these actions have both on ourselves and on other members of our species that share the present with us.

We of the present are also responsible for our actions in the present and the consequences of these actions on all living things that share the present with us.

If we take care to do good in the present,
the future will take care of itself.
Past, present, and future.
Together as one is ...
The Continuum.

THE LEGAL CODE FOR EARTH DEFENDERS

MEDIA LAWS

1. The media is not concerned with facts, figures, statistics or scientific reports. The media is interested in drama, scandal, violence, and sex.

2. Without visuals, there is no story on television. Without photographs, you have a weak story in the print media.

3. Learn to use the media or you will be abused by the media. Media manipulation is merely a matter of survival in a media culture.

4. Always talk in sound bites. Keep it simple. Do not clarify. Never over-estimate the intelligence of the viewer, the listener or the reader.

5. Ignore the question put to you if it does not serve your purpose. Say what you wish to say. Stay in control.

6. Emotion will always triumph over fact. Emote. Use humor. Make the viewer like you.

7. In a media culture, the medium is the message. Television and film are the massage of the mind.

8. Objectivity is a myth, an illusion, a con and a trick. Objectivity in the media does not exist. The illusion of objectivity may work as a strat-egy but only a fool would believe that it is a reality within the media culture.

9. The Media defines reality. What is real is what is reported. The public believes what it is told to believe.

10. Believe nothing that you read, be skeptical about what you hear and question all that you see. All of your senses can be manipulated. You must armor yourself with a healthy dose of doubt. Always question and investigate yourself. Accept nothing in a story without personal inquiry.

THE LAWS OF ECOLOGY

There are five laws of ecology:

1. The Law of Interdependence.
2. The Law of Biological Diversity.
3. The Law of Finite Resources.
4. The Law which states that a Species may not Defecate in a Communal Water-hole. Or Thou Shalt Not Pollute Thy Neighbor's Habitat.
5. The Law of Species Preservation over the interests of an individual or group of individuals of a single species.

THE LAWS OF ECO-GUERRILLA ACTIVITY

(More details in Chapter 11)

1. Do NOT get caught.

2. Silence is imperative.

3. Write nothing down.

4. Do not participate in any action with any individual unless you have known the person for seven years. Make no exceptions.

5. Never participate in a covert or illegal activity with your wife or husband, boyfriend, girlfriend or lover. This is a potentially unstable relationship with a potential for high risk.

6. If caught, remember: NOBODY TALKS—EVERYBODY WALKS.

7. And: NOBODY SIGNS—EVERYTHING'S FINE.

8. NEVER ADMIT NUTHIN.

9. Never burden your supporters. Insure yourself. Provide for bail and legal defenses.

10. Be psychologically, physiologically and emotionally prepared for confrontation and the stress of covert operations.

1

PREPARATIONS

Animis Opibusque Parati *
Semper Paratus **

Strategy is of paramount importance to the ecological activist and to the environmental movement. Strategy is what decides the outcome of an action, a campaign, or an initiative. It is the superiority of a strategy which determines success over failure, freedom over incarceration, or life over death.

It is essential that all ecological activists be schooled in the art of strategy. Failure to know strategy is irresponsible. Failure to understand strategy may result in injury, imprisonment, or death, to yourself, your followers, or your allies. Worse, failure to comprehend strategy can lead to failure and thus further destruction to the environment and/or its inhabitants.

It would be better for the environment and the environmental movement if a person did nothing rather than attempt to carry out a campaign with no strategy, an incomplete strategy, or an inferior strategy.

> The arrests and convictions of the Squamish Five in Canada and the Arizona Five in the United States on charges of sabotage are both examples of failures in strategy which have resulted in severe penalties for both the individuals involved and the environmental movement in general.

All strategy requires the careful and meticulous laying of plans.

All strategy is governed by five constant factors, all of which need to be taken into account and studied thoroughly.

Sun Tzu described these factors as **Moral Law, Environment, Situation, Command, and Method and Discipline.**

* Latin: Animis opibusque parati means, "prepared in minds and resources." ** Semper paratus means, "always ready." Semper paratus is the motto of the U.S. Coast Guard.

The **MORAL LAW** means that your cause must be honest and just. You must be morally superior to your enemy. This is often called taking the moral high ground. If you have and can hold the moral high ground, your followers will follow and your allies will support you, regardless of the risks, and undaunted by danger.

In the environmental movement there are two kinds of moral advantages to take into consideration. For your own followers, those who possess the biocentric outlook of the Earth Warrior, it is important that you remain virtuous in your adherence to biocentric principles. As long as your followers are satisfied with the consistent nature of your philosophical foundation, it is then irrelevant how your views are manifested within the strategy projected.

You have two distinct minds. Use both. Your worldly mind will understand the justification for deception in the presentation of your arguments. Your universal mind, the real you, can remain at peace with the knowledge that your deception has only served to deceive your enemies and not yourself or your allies.

Deception is a weapon. Do not direct it towards your friends and, most importantly, beware of self-deception.

Because we are working within an anthropocentric society, we must be aware of the anthropocentric moral high ground. We must be prepared to present a higher anthropocentric moral stance that makes sense to our opponents, but is in fact, more biocentric in nature.

When opportune, you must appear to be more Christian than the Christians, more humanistic than the humanists, more patriotic than the patriots, etc. This involves being thoroughly schooled in anthropocentric, philosophical thoughts and beliefs. All biocentrists must strive to attain a complete understanding of anthropocentric thought. A good strategist must be able to favorably use the opposition's philosophical arguments.

Praise the Lord and wrap yourself in the flag if this is what it takes to get your message across. It has worked for George Bush— it can just as easily work for you.

Environmentalists too often assume that they are right and that environmentalism is inherently just. It must be remembered however, that justice is a matter of perception. People see what they want to see and hear what they want to hear. What is just and right in the mind of an individual or group may not be just or right in the opinions of others or the general opinion of the public as represented by politicians and influenced by the media.

> *"Print technology created the public.*
> *Electric technology created the mass.*
> *The public consists of separate individuals*
> *walking around with separate fixed points of view.*
> *The new technology demands that we abandon*
> *the luxury of this posture, this fragmentary outlook."*
> **- Marshall McLuhan**

To an Earth Warrior, the biocentric attitudes are both right and just. To society at large, biocentrism is an aberration. You must package your moral superiority in an attractive anthropocentric wrapper.

Within the environmental and especially the animal rights movement, cults of superiority have been established. Vegan proselytizing and pagan mother Goddess worship may serve to unify small mutual interest cliques, but tends to be very alienating to the populace as a whole. In other words, you should not confuse your projected strategy with rhetoric on witchcraft, paganism, anarchism, new age philosophy, and other minority points of view. Nor should you alienate the anthropocentric public by dressing and behaving in a manner which threatens the majority morality.

I am not dictating here that you must dress and conform to the values of the anthropocentric establishment. I am simply pointing out the reality of the consequences should you not do so. When preaching to the Romans, it pays to look and behave like a Roman. People distrust, dislike, and often detest those who appear to be different.

However, if you judge an audience to be receptive to a biocentric approach, then proceed. Or, if you judge that a biocentric approach may shock your audience in a positive way in order to provoke thought, then do proceed.

An educated audience will be more receptive to biocentrism than an uneducated audience.

If you proceed in the advancement of biocentric thought then you must be able to explain your position with knowledge and with spirit. An intellectual understanding of biocentrism is insufficient. You must intuitively understand human existence within the context of the biosphere. You must understand the principles of ecology and of natural laws. You must be able to feel the rhythm of the seasons, sense the phases of the moon, and be attuned to the forces emanating from the Earth and from Life.

It is not enough to know that your cause is just. You must convince the public that it is more just than your opponent's cause. The other side will attempt to espouse the morality of their position by citing the need for jobs, tradition, cultural values, or by appealing to a community and creating a we versus them attitude. Your opposition will attempt to smear you with derogatory labels. You must be prepared for these attacks and counter the public relations machinery and strategies of your opponent.

Where possible, turn the strategy of your opponent back on your opponent. If a developer uses the promise of jobs to obtain leverage, then point out the health hazards posed to children if relevant, or point out that the jobs are just short term and taxes will rise to pay for the development of utilities.

Never appear too serious, but at the same time be thoughtful. Use wit and humor but never appear too humorous. Do not be cynical. Never speak directly to your opponent, but use your conversation or debate to address the public at large. At the same time, do not appear to be discourteous to your opponent. Never lose your temper in public. Be calm, project confidence, and never be at a loss for an answer.

The nature of the mass media today is such that the truth is irrelevant. What is true and what is right to the general public is what is defined as true and right by the mass media. Ronald Reagan understood that the facts are not relevant. The media reported what he said as fact. Follow-up investigation was "old news". A headline comment in Monday's newspaper far outweighs the revelation of inaccuracy revealed in a small box inside the paper on Tuesday or Wednesday.

> *"All media work us over completely. They are*
> *so persuasive in their personal, political, economic,*
> *aesthetic, psychological, moral, ethical, and social*
> *consequences that they leave no part of us untouched,*
> *unaffected, unaltered. The medium is the massage.*
> *Any understanding of social and cultural change is*
> *impossible without a knowledge of the way*
> *media works as environments."*
> **- Marshall McLuhan**

If you do not know an answer, a fact, or a statistic, then simply follow the example of an American President and do as Ronald Reagan did—make it up on the spot and deliver the information confidently and without hesitation.

Concentrate on creating symbols for an issue and appeal to the public through these symbols. Powerful symbols are human babies, children, baby animals, beautiful animals, trees, plants, or landscapes. Emphasize the noble, the beautiful, and the innocent. Do not be abstract.

KEEP IT SIMPLE!

If the issue is polluted water or pesticides, utilize the image of children whose health will be threatened. If the issue is wildlife, focus on the cute, the noble, or the beautiful—appeal to anthropocentric preconceived notions. If the issue is habitat, choose an animal that represents that habitat and accentuate its beauty and nobility. As an example, if the issue is Central American rainforests, then employ the image of the jaguar in your campaign. In Antarctica, use the penguin; in Africa, the elephant. Remember, you will have little success in mobilizing public concern for the mugwort, the saltwater crocodile, the periwinkle, or the shark. Subtlety attach the cause of the less appealing to the public campaign to protect the more appealing. Saving tuna is as important as saving dolphins, but dolphins are more appealing. A campaign to protect dolphins will automatically raise public awareness about tuna. Both species benefit from a campaign to protect one.

Be prepared to recruit celebrities to speak for and support your cause. Celebrities are noticed by the public and can effectively influence the public.

Always prepare an effective media strategy.

Play the media by utilizing the rules established by the mass media. Remember that the media is not interested in the content of your news. The media is interested in the delivery. Drama, not data. Scandal and sex, not statistics. Violence and visuals, not viewpoint. Despite media pretensions, facts are not a priority for most media.

> *"Societies have always been shaped more by*
> *the nature of the media by which men communicate*
> *than by the content of the communication."*
> ### - Marshall McLuhan

Never acknowledge a public relations strategy aimed at you, this simply gives increased credibility to your opponent. You must try to find a way to counter any strategy hat your enemy puts forth.

Always appear before the media as confident, knowledgeable, in control, and in command. Never debate defensively in the media or in public.

Strive to be the David to your opponent's Goliath. There is a moral advantage to being the underdog. Never appear too powerful, too wealthy, or too strong. Keep any power, wealth, or strength hidden and in reserve. Bait the opponent in, and if you still cannot achieve victory, then unleash your reserves.

> *"It is said the warrior's way is the twofold way*
> *of pen and sword."*
> ### - Miyamoto Musashi, 1648.

> *"The way of the Earth warrior is the twofold way*
> *of camera and confrontation."*
> ### - Captain Paul Watson, 1984.

ENVIRONMENT means you must incorporate into your planning the following: night and day, cold and heat, times and seasons.

Always consider proper clothing, equipment, and means of transportation. Do not be caught unprepared for climate or a lack of visibility. Keep a close account of time and strive to be punctual.

Avoid adverse conditions when defending. Exploit adverse conditions when attacking.

Calculate the advantages of fog or darkness for cloaking your approach. Be aware of the phases of the moon. Always approach out of the sun.

Be prepared for parasites, poisonous insects, reptiles, and dangerous animals and plants. Respect these citizens of the wilderness and seek to understand them. All beings within nature should be looked upon as allies. Work with them and not against them.

Learn and understand the nature of herbs in healing. Learn the types of plants that can provide nourishment. Know how to survive in the wilderness or upon the ocean. Be aware of the plants and animals in any area that you are operating.

Be familiar with the geography and the geology of any area in which you are operating. Is the ground sandy, rocky, or composed of clay? Where are the sources of water? Is there firewood? Which way is the wind blowing? Is there a danger of flooding? Does the air smell of coming rain or snow? Be prepared.

When operating in urban areas it is important to know the map. Can you find your way around the city or town? Do you know where the hospital is? The police station? The fire department? Are you familiar with the transportation system? Do you know which areas of town are dangerous to your objectives? Do you have an escape route? Do you have a cover? Do you have an alibi? Is your position adequately protected?

The theory of **SITUATION** means that you must incorporate into your planning the following: distances, danger and security, open ground and narrow passes, high and low ground, and the chances for life and death, injury or capture.

Do you have the means to cover distances? Do you have valid travel documents? Are you prepared for danger? Have you undertaken proper preparations for security? In the event of an accident or attack, have you made arrangements for medical and life insurance? Do you have an up-to-date and valid will? These are very important considerations. Failure to insure yourself will burden your followers and allies.

COMMAND signifies leadership. Leaders must possess wisdom, intuition, sincerity, resourcefulness, and benevolence tempered with strictness and courage.

There are nine types of leaders:

There are leaders who guide with virtue and treat all equally and with courtesy. Such a leader is aware of the conditions of followers and takes notice of their troubles. Such leaders are called humanistic.

Example:**Randy Hayes** *(Rainforest Action Network)*

There are leaders who do not avoid any task and are not influenced by profit. Such a leader places honour above self and is called a dutiful leader.

Example: **Helen Caldicott** *(Physicians for Nuclear Responsibility)*

There are leaders who do not allow themselves to become arrogant because of their high position. Such a leader does not make much of their victories, but remains wise and humble and continues to be both strong and tolerant. These are leaders of courtesy.

Example: **John Seed** *(Rainforest Information Center)*

There are leaders whose actions are unpredictable and unknowable, whose movements and responses are varied. Such a leader can turn impending defeat into victory. These are the clever leaders.

Example: **David Brower** *(Earth Island Institute)*

There are leaders whose lives set an example for others. Such leaders are the saints of the environmental movement and a source of inspiration.

Example: **Thomas Berry** *(Author—A Dream of Earth)*

There are leaders who lead their followers into the field. Such a leader displays courage and skills in confrontation. These are field leaders.

Example: **Chico Mendes** *(Brazilian activist —murdered 1988)*

There are leaders who face the overwhelming odds and dangers of campaigns, displaying no fear and remaining calm. Such leaders are always in the front during an advance and in the rear guard during withdrawal. These are frontline leaders.

Example: **Mike Roselle** *(Earth First!)*

There are leaders who have a gift for communication, who understand and can manipulate the media. These are charismatic leaders.

Example: **Robert Hunter** *(Greenpeace Founder)*

There are leaders whose skill, tactics, and courage strike fear and loathing in the hearts of the opposition. Such leaders never spurn good advice and are always both humble and firm. These are uncomplicated men and women yet they have numerous strategies. These are great leaders.

Example: **David Foreman** *(Wild Earth Society)*

TALENTS OF LEADERSHIP

To detect treachery and danger.

To win the allegiance of others.

To be able to rise early in the morning and to retire late.

To speak words that are discreet yet perceptive.

To be direct yet circumspect.

To have courage and the will to fight.

To be of martial bearing and to be fierce of heart.

To understand the hardship of others and to guard against exposing followers to cold and hunger.

To be trustworthy and just.

To be able to understand the mass psychology of the general public and to understand media tactics for communicating with the general public.

To be able to read the signs of the sky, the earth, the sea, and the stars.

To protect all beings and to protect the Earth by understanding that all is one.

To display maternal affection for all living beings.

To lead with the heart, plan with the mind, fight with the body, and triumph with the spirit.

"90 percent of success is just showing up."
-Woody Allen

(In other words, be active not reactive, get off your ass and get involved. Take the initiative. Stand up and be there.)

EVILS OF LEADERSHIP

"Wealth should come like manna from
heaven, unearned and uncalled for. Money should
be like grace - a gift. It is not worth sweating and
scheming for."
- Edward Abbey

Never be greedy.

Never be jealous or envious of those who are wiser, more able, or more wealthy.

Never make friends with the treacherous or believe the words of the slanderous.

Never judge others without judging yourself.

Never be hesitant or indecisive.

Never be influenced by flattery or take advice from sycophants.

Never be heavily addicted to alcohol, drugs, or sex.

Never lie with malice or have a cowardly heart.

Never boast wildly and never talk without courtesy.

Never be close-minded.

SKILLS OF LEADERSHIP

To know the disposition and power of the enemy.

To know how to approach and withdraw from the enemy.

To know how weak or how strong your opposition is.

To know the ways of nature and human psychology.

To know the geography, the terrain, and the situation in the theater of operations.

THE VICE OF ARROGANCE IN LEADERS

Leaders should never be arrogant. Arrogance leads to discourtesy. Discourtesy will alienate followers and allies. Alienation leads to rebellion.

By **METHOD AND DISCIPLINE** you must understand the importance of arranging your forces. You must understand how to delegate responsibility. You must understand maintenance of your forces. You must also understand how to manage your expenditures, your resource base.

To properly plan a campaign for victory, the following questions must be answered:

Is your position morally superior to your enemy according to society values and morales?

Which side has the best leadership?

Which side has the advantages of natural and situational circumstances?

Which side is most positively motivated?

Which side rewards its followers better? Which side is most just in administering discipline?

On whose side are the leaders and the followers more highly trained and experienced?

Which side is the stronger?

Which side has the better media strategy?

These considerations will decide in advance if a campaign will win or lose.

Within the environmental movement there are four working structures.

These are individuals, action groups, organizations, and coalitions.

An individual structure is concerned with the path of the infiltrator and the saboteur. It should be covert and low profile. Leadership is singular and personal, and responsibility involves only the individual.

An Action Group is a small active unit operating on its own or on behalf of an organization. There should be a field leader. If acting on behalf of an organization there should be an organizational leader to whom the field leader reports. Action groups may be low or high profile depending upon the strategy employed.

An Organization must have a good administrator and it must have a clearly defined chain of command as well as a listing of responsibilities. Organizations may only act overtly. Covert action must be delegated to an Action Group.

The most effective political approach is to link organizations into coalitions. The danger here is that the strategy set by a Coalition may only be as strong as the weakness member of the coalition. It is possible however for a stronger group to manipulate member organizations into supporting a stronger approach. Use diplomacy and deception if necessary.

DECEPTION

All confrontation is based on deception. This is called the strategy of tactical paradox.

When you are able to attack, you must seem unable.

When you are active, you should appear inactive.

When you are near, you should have the enemy believe you are far. And when far, near.

Bait the enemy.

Pretend to be disorganized, then strike.

If the enemy is secure, then be prepared.

If the enemy be of superior strength, then evade.

If your opponent has a weakness of temper, then strive to irritate.

Make a pretense of being weak and cultivate your opponent's arrogance.

If your opponent is at ease, then ensure that they are given no rest.
If the forces of your opponent are united, then seek to divide them.
Attack when the enemy is unprepared.
Appear when you are not expected.
The leader who wins makes careful plans.

Even an intuitive strategy without design or concept should be a part of an overall plan.

Preparing plans is an important factor in the Art of Strategy when it is applied to the service of the Biosphere.

Preparation for Death.

> *"The Way of the warrior is resolute acceptance of death."*
> **- Miyamoto Musashi, 1648.**

The Earth warrior, like all warriors, must be prepared for death. Live each day fully as if it were your last.

Do not burden your soul with unfinished business. Be at peace with those you love. Honor your friends and cherish your loves.

Watch your enemies and be vigilant but never surrender to fear.

The knowledge of the inevitability of your death coupled with your acceptance of death will allow you the freedom to proceed and to fight without fear.

> *"Hoka hey"*
>
> **- Lakota** *meaning:"It's a good day to die."*

2

CONFRONTATION

Vi Et Armis*

The longer the confrontation, the greater the expense.

The longer a confrontation lasts, the more followers will be lost from fatigue and disenchantment.

Conflict is like a fire. If you do not put it out, it will burn itself out, but only after it consumes the participants.

If a confrontation lasts too long, your strength will be diminished.

The longer a confrontation lasts, the more dissension there will be in your ranks. Dissension can lead to rebellion by your own forces against you.

Prolonged confrontation is not a wise strategy.

Instead, maneuver your opposition into fighting a prolonged campaign. Keep up a continued token resistance if need be. Expend energy and resources in short bursts only. Attack and retreat, attack and retreat.

Wear down the enemy with hit and run tactics if you find that victory cannot be swift and decisive.

Tree-spiking and monkey-wrenching tactics are excellent hit and run tactics. Strike from the shadows and then disappear into the shadows.

The forces of environmentalism are small. The only strategy for conflict against corporate power, mass media propaganda, and anthropocentric attitudes is a strategy of attack and retreat.

Remember, environmentalists must have no illusion about decisive victory or even victory in our lifetime. We are simply buying time for the future. Our superior ally is the Earth herself and the forces of apocalypse that she will muster against the oppression of human arrogance.

Do not make haste with your plans, but do not delay once your plans have been translated into action.

You must calculate the time and means of your victory in advance.

* Latin: Vi et armis means "by force of arms."

Being ahead in your timing is the single most important factor in obtaining a victory.

The environmental movement has been, for the most part, a reactive movement. Rarely has there been campaigns where the advance of the enemy against the ecosystem were anticipated and countered before the enemy had moved.

Do not wait for an area to be declared as a target for a forest clear-cut. Spike the trees years in advance. This will counter forest industry and government security measures and it will better disguise the evidence of spiking. In addition, you will be ready to retaliate to an announcement of proposed logging with a press release stating that protective measures for the trees have already been taken.

Activities by environmentalists are for the most part a series of small, inexpensive skirmishes against a powerful, better equipped opposition. A direct face to face encounter will almost always result in failure because of the superior financial resources of the opposition. A prolonged face to face campaign on open ground will certainly result in failure. The way of the Earth Warrior is to rely on the covert attack, the surprise attack, and planned defense security.

The second most important factor is resourcefulness. You must be prepared to survive in the field. Recruit crewmembers with good foraging and scrounging skills.

My ships are a collection of materials from around the world, all obtained from ports of call and all obtained freely. From waste bins, from abandoned buildings, from derelict ships, from Naval yards, from supporters. My crew of scroungers, rievers, and resourceful opportunists has saved us thousands of dollars in parts, supplies, and essential equipment.

Also, when possible, seize, utilize, and exploit the materials, tools, intelligence, and weapons of the opposition.

Your financial supporters want results, not excuses. They won't support you if you should fail and continue to use the same strategy and tactics. They will not support you for a prolonged period of time unless progress is made. Victories must be achieved. Checkmates win acclaim. Stalemates will bore your supporters. Losses will deplete some or all of your support. In conflict it is important to win and win swiftly. It is better to win one skirmish after another than to have a prolonged conflict. Hope is built on decision, courage, and action.

It is important that your followers are rewarded for their opposition to the enemy. These rewards may be material or spiritual. If material, the rewards must be distributed fairly.

Never expose yourself to direct interception without first preparing a strategy to escape.

Most importantly, remember that if you are visibly effective and leave yourself open to attack, you WILL be taken out by the opposition—without question.

Thus the more effective you become in visibly hurting the opposition, the lower you must keep your public profile. The only other defense is to increase your public profile to the status of celebrity. The opposition must then weigh the advantages and disadvantages of public reaction to your removal.

If a major environmental organization is more powerful than the targeted opposition in terms of money, numbers, and political clout, it is important that the group deploy strategies with tact and diplomacy. A crushing victory may result in a moral backlash if an environmental David is perceived as a Goliath.

Be subtle, never heavy handed. Display compassion, sympathy, and understanding. Never come off as uncaring or bureaucratic. Bureaucracy in itself is an enemy. Never allow the infiltration of uncontrollable bureaucracy into your ranks.

Leaders must never surrender control to a bureaucracy.

Confrontations must be in the control of a defined leadership. When confrontation begins, the time for democratic discussion of strategy and tactics has ended. All decisions must then be entrusted to a recognized command.

"When this ship becomes a democracy,
you'll be the first to know."
　　　　- **Captain James T. Kirk**
　　　　to a crewmember on the Starship Enterprise

Many groups use the method of democratic consensus in decision making. This is not wise, but if this is the way accepted by the group, then it should always be consensus less one. There is a psychology of some individuals who will block a decision simply for the sense of power that it gives them. In fact, some of these individuals often seek out such groups for this purpose. Their priorities lie in dealing with their own psychological problems and not with the issues at hand.

Consensus always arrives at a decision which is most compatible with the weakest individual participating.

Leadership should be organic, springing from the ground with passion, courage, skill, imagination, and ideas.

Leadership should give birth to tactics and strategy.

Tactics and strategy defined and controlled by a group effort will always be devoid of the passion of leadership and mitigated to the point of ineffectiveness.

"You must know something about strategy and
tactics and logistics, but also economics and politics
and diplomacy and history. You must know everything
you can know about military power, and you must
also understand the limits of military power."
　　　　- **John F. Kennedy,** *June 7, 1961*
　　　　U.S. Naval Academy Commencement Speech.

In direct confrontation—never compromise. In indirect confrontation—use compromise as a tactic of deception only.

The Earth Warrior must never compromise in defense of the Earth.

3

THE ART OF FIGHTING WITHOUT FIGHTING

Vis Consili Expers Mole Ruit Sua *

To fight and conquer in all your battles is not true excellence. Instead, excellence should consist of breaking the enemy's resistance without fighting. In the practical art of war, the best thing of all is to take the enemy's country whole and intact; to shatter and destroy it is counter productive. So, too, it is better to capture an army entire than to destroy it, or to capture a regiment, a detachment, or a company rather than destroying them. In the environmental movement it is imperative that victories be realized without causing or sustaining injuries or fatalities.

Thus the highest form of leadership is to foil the enemies plans; the next best thing is to prevent the unification of the enemy's forces—to interfere with your enemy's alliances, to divide and conquer. The next is to subvert your enemy's strategy. The last resort is to openly engage in conflict.

The worst policy of all is to besiege. To besiege is to prolong the time and to maximize the expenses. This should be avoided at all costs.

The skillful leader subdues the enemy's forces without fighting: they capture without laying siege and they overthrow without lengthy operations in the field. With forces intact the skillful leader disputes the mastery of the opponent, and thus, without losing any forces, the triumph is complete.

This is the method of attacking by stratagem, of using the sheathed sword.

In the rule in conflict, if your forces are ten to one, then surround the enemy. If twice as many, divide into two forces, one to meet the enemy in front, and one to fall upon the rear. If the enemy replies to the frontal attack, defeat will come from behind; if the attack is from the rear, defeat will come from the front.

If equally matched, offer battle; if slightly inferior in number, then avoid the enemy. If completely unequal in every way, then retreat fully.

*Latin: Vis Consili expers mole ruit sua means literally, "force without good sense falls by its own weight." A modern translation would be, "discretion is the better part of valor."

Using guerrilla tactics, unequal numbers may be substituted with stealth, maneuverability, and hit and run tactics to allow you equal or better odds.

The leader is the bulwark of the campaign: if the bulwark is strong at all points, the campaign will be strong; if the bulwark is defective, the campaign will be weakened.

There are three ways that a leader can bring defeat to a campaign:

1. By commanding followers to advance or to retreat, when there are economic or physical barriers which may make it impossible to obey. This is called "hobbling" your followers.

2. A leader of a military, political, or environmental campaign cannot govern their forces in the same way that citizens are governed by a benevolent state. Humanity and justice are the principles on which to govern a benevolent state, but not an army or parts thereof. Opportunism and flexibility are civic rather than military virtues. To govern your forces in a non-military manner will cause restlessness and division within your followers.

3. A leader must not employ officers or delegate authority without discrimination or without heed to military principle of adaptation to circumstances. This shakes the confidence of your followers.

If a leader is ignorant of the principle of adaptability, then they must not be entrusted with a position of authority. The skillful employer of people will employ the wise person, the brave person, the covetous person, and the stupid person. The wise person delights in establishing merit, the brave person likes to show courage in action, the covetous person is quick at seizing advantages, and the stupid person may have no fear of death.

You should not allow your followers to become restless and distrustful. Do not allow anarchy to breed among your followers.

There are five essentials for victory:

1. You will win if you know when to fight and when not to fight.

2.   You will win if you know how to handle both superior and inferior forces.

3. You will win if your followers are animated by the same spirit throughout all their ranks.

4. You will win if you are prepared and your enemy is unprepared.

5. You will win if you have the strategic capacity to not be interfered with in the field by your sovereign body, i.e government, corporate board, etc.

If you know the enemy and know yourself, you will triumph.

If you know yourself but not the enemy, for every victory you win, you will also suffer a defeat. If you know neither the enemy nor yourself, you will be defeated in every battle.

Fighting Your Allies

The environmental movement is composed of numerous individuals, action groups, organizations, and coalitions. These factions promote different agendas and promote different strategies for achieving their objectives.

It is beneficial in a movement to promote harmony so as to direct the greater force against the primary opposition.

If factions have different strategies, they should seek to agree to disagree on tactics and objectives. If this fails, use diplomacy to manipulate a mutual non-aggression policy. If this fails, then use agents to infiltrate, undermine, and if need be, subtlety destroy your opposing "ally".

Unless it is unavoidable, do not publicly battle an ally. This will only serve the interest of the primary opposition.

If your organization or action group is infiltrated by people promoting a different agenda then isolate these voices through ridicule and non-coopera-tion. Treat them as you would treat the enemy.

If the infiltration becomes strong, this means that you failed in your organizational leadership. The solution here is to abandon the organization and regroup.

As an example, in 1990, Earth First! became seriously divided between the original deep ecology faction and those who later joined with a leftist, feminist, and liberal social agenda. The infiltrators went so far as to denounce an essential Earth First! tenet which advocates monkey-wrenching.

Earth First! co-founder, Dave Foreman, turned the tables on the infiltrators by resigning from the organization and founding a new group called Wild Earth.

As Foreman put it: "If you live in a mansion, you're going to fight to keep it. But if you live in an Apache wikkiup, when the vermin move in, well, then you simply move out."

> *I kill an ant*
> *realize my children*
> *have been watching.*
>
> **- Haiku, Shuson** *(19th Century)*

Turn all attacks upon you into strategies of retaliation. Use the force of your enemy's charge and turn it back upon your enemy. Use your enemy's own arguments and tactics within your strategy. Your enemy, if understood, will provide the key to your victory.

TACTICS

Vincam Aut Moriar *

You must always put yourself beyond the possibility of being defeated and then wait for an opportunity to defeat the enemy.

> *"Give me a fair ship so that I might go into harm's way."*
> **- John Paul Jones**

To secure yourself against defeat lies in your own hands, but the opportunity of defeating the enemy is provided by the enemy themselves. Hence the saying: One may know how to conquer without being able to do it.

Security against defeat implies defensive tactics; the ability to defeat the enemy means taking the offensive. Standing on the defensive indicates insufficient strength; attacking indicates an abundance of strength.

The leader who is skilled in defense hides in the dark; the leader who is skilled in offense charges forth from the sky. Thus, on the one hand, we have the ability to protect ourselves; on the other, to gain a complete victory.

To see victory only when it is within the understanding of the average person is not excellence. Nor is it excellence if you fight and win and you are rewarded. True excellence is to plan secretly, to move surreptitiously, to foil the enemy's intentions, and to thwart their schemes. The victory can be won without shedding a drop of blood.

A clever tactician is one who not only wins, but excels in winning with ease. A clever tactician will find that victories will bring neither a reputation for wisdom nor credit for courage. Victories gained by circumstances that will not come to light will mean that the world at large will know nothing of them.

A master of tactics will be satisfied with the achievement of plans and unconcerned about public reward. This same tactician wins by making no

* Latin: Vincam Aut Moriar means " I will conquer or die."

mistakes. Making no mistakes is what establishes the certainty of victory, for it means conquering an enemy that is already defeated.

Thus the skillful tactician will put themselves into a position that makes defeat impossible and does not miss the moment for defeating the enemy. Thus it is that in conflict the victorious strategist seeks battle only after the victory has been won. The strategist destined for defeat is the one who first fights and afterward looks for victory.

The excellent leader cultivates moral law and strictly adheres to method and discipline. Thus, it is in their power to control success.

APPLICATION OF TACTICS

For the Earth Warrior, tactical approaches will include the following:

> 1. Field Tactics.
> 2. Media Tactics.
> 3. Psychological Tactics.
> 4. Educational Tactics.
> 5. Intuitive Tactics.

1. Field Tactics: For environmental activists, these tactics are known as "monkey-wrenching." These are tactics of sabotage, covert activity, and direct action. The recommended manual for the study of field tactics in the environmental movement is *Eco-Defense—The Field Guide to Monkey-Wrenching,* by Dave Foreman. These are tactics to be utilized by the Catalyst and the Infiltrator. These tactics require courage, stealth, and skill in the practical application of tactics, and the knowledge of laws and tactics of evasion.

2. Media Tactics: In the realm of eco-warfare, the camera is much more powerful than the sword. Documentation and investigation are powerful tactical approaches. A study of the philosophy of Marshall McLuhan is valuable. All eco-warriors should be knowledgeable in the use of cameras,

especially video cameras. A reading of Robert Hunter's book *Warriors Of The Rainbow* will illustrate the advantage of an environmental group skillfully manipulating the media. These are tactics to be utilized by the Communicator, the Catalyst, and the Shaman. These tactics require skills in speaking, writing, photography, media, and control.

3. Psychological Tactics: A foundation in understanding the psychology of humans and human institutions will be valuable in the manipulation and deception of organizations and individuals. It will also serve in implementing the valuable tactic of divide and conquer. These are tactics to be utilized by the Infiltrator, the Communicator, the Shaman, the Artist, and the Catalyst. These tactics require a knowledge of psychology.

4. Educational Tactics: Utilize the media and direct involvement to reach and influence people and advance your position. These are long-term tactics but overall they are the most essential for realizing a permanent change in attitudes. These are tactics to be utilized by the Communicator, the Artist, the Healer, the Shaman, and the Catalyst. These tactics require skills in media, education, and patience.

5. Intuitive Tactics: These are tactics to be found when the Earth Warrior touches the Earth and is given the tactics directly. These are the tactics to be employed when implementing Musashi's strategy of No Design, No Concept. These tactics are available only if you are intuitively connected to the Earth.

> *"When you realize the value of all life, you dwell less on what is past and concentrate more on the preservation of the future."*
>
> **- Dian Fossey**
> *Last entry in her journal the night she was murdered.*

5

EARTHFORCE

Vis Consili Expers Mole Ruit Sua *

The control of a large force is the same in principle as the control of a small group; it is simply a question of dividing up their numbers. It is a matter of preparation and organization.

Organize a chain of command. In this way, one may command the many. To manage a few is to manage millions.

Divide your followers into ordinary and extraordinary. Use your ordinary followers to engage. Use your extraordinary followers to achieve victory.

The environmental movement is composed of moderate and extremists factions. Utilize both. Use the moderates for direct attacks and the extremists for indirect attacks. Use the moderates for overt activities. Use the extremists for covert activities.

Just as nation states maintain both overt and covert control, so must any effective movement operate through the utilization of both covert and overt units.

To ensure that your force will withstand the brunt of the enemy's attack and remain unshaken, use maneuvers that are direct and indirect. Direct methods may be used in joining battle, but indirect methods will be needed in order to secure a victory.

Environmentalists operating as individuals, action groups, or as an organization can be attacked both directly and indirectly by the government. Directly by the police in response to (a) a real crime or (b) a bogus crime or indirectly by the police utilizing a "sting" strategy. The government can also strike indirectly through taxing agencies. Organizations and individuals can come under investigation and harassment by government taxing agencies. Your defense is overtly to keep proper books or covertly to not leave a paper trail.

* Latin: Vis consili expers mole ruit sua means "discretion is the better part of valor. Literally "force without good sense falls by its own weight." Quotation from Horace's *Odes*.

The nature of a government attack can be determined by your own strategy.

If you utilize covert or illegal tactics, you can expect any direct or indirect strategies from government forces, including your own assassination. Your only defense lies in secrecy, careful planning and vigilance.

If you utilize civil disobedience, you will be directly attacked and arrested. Your defense is through established legal channels. You must be prepared.

If you operate openly you need to be prepared for the possibility of being set up. Be prepared to have a defense. Remember, if you operate overtly, keep a record of all activities and maintain accurate accounting. In other words, keep your nose clean. Be prepared to defend yourself in the courts and in the media. For the overt strategy, the courts and the media are the primary battlefields.

If you operate covertly, do not keep any records of real activities. Do not leave a paper trail of any kind. The covert warrior strives to stay off the legal battlefields. The media may be used tactically, but the covert strategy is indirect and difficult to defend if attacked directly.

Direct action speaks louder than words.

Indirect tactics, efficiently applied, are inexhaustible, limited only by the imagination of the tactician.

In conflict, there are two methods of attack: the direct and the indirect. Yet these two in combination give rise to an endless series of tactical maneuvers. The direct and the indirect lead on to each other in turn. It is like moving in a circle, you never come to an end. The possibilities of combination cannot be exhausted.

The good fighting force must be terrifying in its onslaught and prompt in decision.

The good fighting force must go into conflict mean and come out clean.

An effective environmental action group must be ruthless in its pursuit and quick with decisions.

Direction may be compared to the bending of a bow, decision to releasing the arrow.

Amid the turmoil and tragedy of conflict, there may be seeming disorder and yet no real disorder. Amid confusion and chaos, your force may be without head or tail, yet it will still be proof against defeat. Simulated disorder postulates perfect discipline, simulated fear postulates courage, and simulated weakness postulates strength. Hiding order beneath the cloak of disorder is simply a question of subdividing. Concealing courage under a show of fear or timidity presupposes a stock of latent energy. Masking strength with weakness is to be effected by tactical dispositions.

In brief, if you wish to feign cowardice, you must possess considerable courage. If you wish to feign weakness, you must possess considerable strength. If you wish to feign disorder, you must possess considerable order.

If you wish to keep the enemy on the move, you must maintain deceitful appearances, according to which the enemy will act. You must sometimes sacrifice something so that the enemy can snatch at it. You must hold out baits, keep the enemy on the go and then, with a well organized move, lie in wait for a mistake.

During the month of March 1983, I used my ship to blockade the harbour entrance to the Port of St. John's, Newfoundland in Canada. The objective was to prevent the Canadian sealing fleet from departing.

Although I had no intention of attacking any sealing ships, I stated that I would ram the first sealer that left the harbour. It was an aggressive bluff backed up by a solid reputation that I had already made from ramming ships in the past.

The bluff worked and the sealing ships stayed in port, thus saving 76,000 seals that year.

To keep the government from attacking, I bluffed and deceived and gave the impression of being dangerously unpredictable.

Feigning a move north, I instead moved south and then west, striking at an unanticipated point where I was able to rout three sealing ships and chase them from the seal nurseries. To do so, I hid under cover of the weather.

It took nearly a week before the Canadian authorities were

able to arrest my ship and crew. The arrest however was anticipated and part of my overall strategy to challenge and defeat the laws with which we disagreed, and we succeeded.

The clever strategist looks to the effect of combined energy and does not require too much from single individuals. The leader must however take individual talent into account and utilize each person according to their capabilities. Use people of courage to carry an attack. Use people of caution to defend your position. Use people of intelligence to give counsel. Do not waste talent.

A leader must not demand perfection from the unskilled or the untrained. A leader must expect perfection from those whose training proclaim them to be masters of their craft.

If an unskilled volunteer makes a mistake, the fault lies with the leader. The leader must oversee or appoint a responsible overseer to monitor the unskilled so as to avoid error.

The responsibility for all errors lies with the leader.

A leader cannot demand victory from followers. A skilled strategist prepares properly so as to utilize a situation. It is the situation which must be controlled and exploited.

A good leader will select followers who will best exploit the situation.

The leader uses momentum to march followers forward. Moving the force carries the individuals along. Thus the timid move with the brave. The force moves as one.

A leader must depend on opportunity and expediency in seeking a victory. Take advantage of the situation. There are three situations to look for in this regard: the morale of your followers and of your opposition, the control of the terrain, and how to take advantage of the weakness of your opposition.

When a leader utilizes combined energy, followers become like rolling stones. For it is the nature of a stone to remain motionless on level ground and to move on a slope; if four cornered, to come to a stop, but if rounded, to go rolling downward. Thus the energy developed by trained and well disciplined followers is as the momentum of a round stone rolled down a mountain thousands of metres in height.

Direction of energy and force is the business of strategy. The direction of energy and force is the responsibility of the leader. The direction of energy and force towards the benefit of the Earth is the strategic goal of the Warrior for the Earth.

An Earthforce is an organized fighting force of warriors dedicating their energies towards the objectives of protecting the biosphere. Force and energy plus organization equal an effective Earthforce.

"It is not enough to understand the natural world:
The point is to defend and preserve it."
- Edward Abbey

6

STEALTH AND UNPREDICTABILITY

Certum Est Quia Impossible Est *

If you desire that your impact be like a typhoon or an earthquake, you must understand the visible and the invisible.

When possible, you must be first in the field. The enemy should come to you. If you are not first in the field, do not rush in to do battle. You must ensure that your fighting strength has not been exhausted. You must impose your will upon the enemy. At the same time you must not allow the enemy to impose its will upon you. Sometimes by holding out an advantage to your enemy, you will draw your opponent to you voluntarily; or, by inflicting damage, you can make it impossible for your enemy to draw near. In the first case, entice with a bait; in the second strike at some important point that the enemy will be forced to defend.

If the enemy is taking a rest, harass; if stationary, force your opponent to move; if well supplied with supplies, wait and work to cut off the supplies. Appear at places the enemy must rush to defend, move swiftly to places where you are not expected.

Attack where your opponent cannot defend. Hold positions that cannot be attacked. A leader skilled in attack will force the opponent to not know what to defend. A leader skilled in defense will force the enemy to not know what to attack.

Utilize the arts of subtlety and secrecy. Learn to be invisible. Learn to be inaudible. Fight when you wish to fight. If the enemy is secure, force them to move by attacking at an undefended point. If the enemy wishes to force you to fight, then cut his lines of communication and move around and behind the strong points of your opponent.

If you do not wish to fight, prevent the enemy from engagement. You can do this by throwing something odd and unpredictable in the way.

* Latin: Certum est quia impossible est means "it is certain because it is impossible.

In 1981, two of my crew and I landed on a Siberian beach to document evidence on illegal Soviet whaling activities. We were approached by two Soviet soldiers. I turned my back on them and stepped into our inflatable boat. My crew sat in the bow facing the beach as I slowly motored away from the shore. "What are they doing?" I asked. My photographer replied, "They have their rifles aimed at us. I think they're going to shoot."

"Smile and wave." I replied without looking back. My two crew smiled and waved and I kept my back to them until we were out of range. They did not shoot.

My tactic confused them. They were uncertain of who we were. We acted friendly. They would be punished severely if they made a mistake. It is psychologically dificult to shoot a person in the back who has not demonstrated a threat. It is even more difficult to shoot a person who is smiling and waving at you. At the same time, it was a good risk. I decided to gamble with favorable odds and we won.

Discover the dispositions of your opponent while remaining invisible. You can learn to concentrate your forces while dividing the forces of your opponent.

Divide and conquer. Pit your whole against separate parts of your opponent's whole. To strengthen one part of the whole, another part must be weakened; take advantage of this.

You must choose the place and the time for confrontation. Always seek to place the burden of reaction on your opposition.

If the enemy is superior in numbers, prevent your opponent from fighting. Scheme and discover the plans of your opposition and the likelihood of the success of those plans. Arouse your enemy and learn the principle of activity or inactivity of your opponent. Force the opposition to reveal themselves. Compare your forces with the forces of your opposition so as to determine your own strength and weakness.

In making tactical decisions, the most important factor is to conceal your plans; conceal your dispositions, and you will be safe from the prying of the most subtle spies.

Produce victory out of the enemy's own tactics.

All people can see the individual tactics needed to conquer, but it is more difficult to see the strategy out of which total victory must evolve.

Tactics are like water; for water in its natural course runs away from high places and moves downward. In confrontation, the way is to avoid what is strong and to strike at what is weak. Water shapes its course according to the nature of the ground over which it flows. The warrior works out a victory in relation to the behaviour of the opposition.

Therefore, just as water retains no constant shape, so in confrontation there are no constant conditions. The five elements- water, fire, wood, metal, earth- are not always equally predominant; the four seasons make way for each other in turn. Modify your tactics in relationship to your opponent and you will be a successful captain of tactics and strategy.

> *"Grandiosity has no place in night work.*
> *So stay invisible."*
>
> *-Peg Millett*

7

MANEUVERING

Coelum Non Animun Mutant Qui Trans Mare Currunt *

Without harmony in your organization, no strategic expedition can be undertaken; without harmony within your expeditionary force, no conflict can be won.

In a field conflict, the leader receives commands from the organization. Having collected and concentrated all forces, the leader must blend and harmonize the different elements at command.

After this initial organization comes the tactical maneuvering, and this is the most difficult. The difficulty consists in turning the devious into the direct, and misfortune into gain. For instance, to take a long and circuitous route after enticing the enemy out of the way. Or starting out after the enemy to reach the objective in advance of your opponent. This shows knowledge of the art of deviation.

Maneuvering with a disciplined force is an advantage, with an undisciplined force it is most dangerous. Never set a fully equipped force in its entirety to snatch an advantage, the chances are you will be too late. Detach a flying column and sacrifice baggage and stores. Your full force cannot operate without it's provisions and equipment. A flying column can achieve the advantage without baggage and if lost it can be expendable.

Never enter into an alliance without knowing the designs of your potential ally. Do not send your full force into unknown terrain. Always make use of local guides.

During my seal campaigns to Newfoundland in 1976 and 1977, I hired local guides. I had also dispatched spies to Newfoundland months in advance to scout the terrain and the

---

* Latin: Coelum non animum mutant qui trans mare currunt means "those who cross the sea change the sky, not their spirits." Quotation from Horace's *Epistles*.

temperament of the local population. Prior to launching the campaign, I travelled to Newfoundland myself to assess the situation. These were invaluable precautions.

In conflict, practise dissimulation. Move only if there is a real advantage to be gained. The decision to concentrate or divide your force must be decided by circumstances. Be rapid. Be compact. Raid swiftly and be immovable.

Be sure that your plans are impenetrable.

Ponder and deliberate before you make your move.

Learn the value of communication through signals.

Your followers' spirit will be at its best in the morning. By noon, the spirit will begin to wane and in the evening,it is near gone.Remember this for action.

At the same time, impose your will in the evening when the spirit to resist is weakest.

Do not interfere with your enemy if their forces are returning home. A person whose heart is set upon returning home will fight with determination against any attempt to bar the way. Allow them to retreat.

When you surround an opposing force, always leave a way free for your opponent to retreat. Have your enemy believe that there is an escape route to prevent the strength generated by despair and hopelessness.

Do not put your opposition in a position to be completely humiliated. Humiliation inspires desperation.

Never press a desperate enemy too hard.

Never utilize the same strategy twice in the same situation against the same opposition.

In 1981, I landed an expedition in Soviet Siberia to document evidence of illegal whaling activities. I landed my small crew on the beach, keeping my ship some two miles off shore. My crew began to film and photograph the whaling station in full view of two armed Soviet soldiers. The soldiers did not interfere, they assumed that we must be Soviet scientists or government people. By the time they suspected that we might be illegal, we had obtained the evidence and had returned to the ship. None of my crew were apprehended or hurt.

A couple of years later, the Greenpeace Foundation conducted the same campaign in the same area. Eight people were arrested and charged with espionage. A ninth crew member suffered a broken leg. Their documentation was confiscated. What was a workable strategy in 1981 did not work in 1983. The strategy of surprise cannot be used twice in the same place against the same opposition.

> *"Use anger to throw them into disarray, use humility to make them haughty.*
> *Tire them by flight, cause division among them.*
> *Attack when they are unprepared, make your move when they do not expect it.*
> *Be extremely subtle, even to the point of soundlessness, Thereby you can be the director of the opponent's fate."*
>
> *-Sun Tzu*

MAINTAINING THE CENTER

Virtutis Fortuna Comes *

Do not camp in difficult terrain. Do not linger in isolated positions. In a difficult situation, use strategy, in a desperate situation you must fight.

There are forces that must not be taken on, positions that must not be contested, and commands that must not be obeyed.

Considerations of advantages and of disadvantages must be blended together.

Reduce the leaders opposing you by inflicting damage upon them; make trouble for them, and keep them constantly engaged; hold out allurements, and make them rush about to any given point.

Entice away the enemy's best warriors and counselors. Recruit traitors and introduce spies to weaken the decisions of your opponent. Foment intrigue and deceit, and sow dissension among the enemy leaders and followers. Corrupt the morals of your enemy. Disturb and unsettle the mind of your enemy by using strategy.

Resist reliance on the possibility your enemy will not choose to encounter you. Instead be always prepared to receive your opposition. Do not rely on the chance that you will not be attacked. Rely instead that you have made your position unassailable.

There are five faults that may affect a leader. These are dangerous faults and a leader is weakened by any one of them:

The first is recklessness, which leads to destruction.

The second is cowardice, which leads to capture. The overly cautious leader will also be captured.

The third fault is a delicacy of honour, which is sensitive to shame.

The fourth is a hasty temper, which can be provoked by insults.

The last fault is oversolicitude for your followers, which exposes a leader

* Latin: Virtutis fortuna comes means "good luck is the companion of courage."

to worry and trouble. Keep in mind that in the long run, your followers will suffer more from the defeat in attaining your common goals than they will suffer in striving to attain these same goals.

Keep in mind that your followers will complain. It is in human nature to complain. Satisfy all of the petty complaints and you will take energy away from the primary objective. Followers will not respect a leader who fails regardless of your kindness. Concern and kindness are forgotten by followers when failure results. The leader answers for failure alone. Victory is shared by all. The leader's responsibility is to the objective first. A leader's responsibility to followers is to provide adequate resources for the welfare of followers through delegation of authority. A leader must never become preoccupied with the complaints of followers.

A leader in the field must never give in to demands for democracy. Decisions made are the responsibility of the leader, the consequences fall on his or her head if negative. If positive, the followers share the victory.

> I made the mistake of giving in to my crew's demand to leave the field and went against my judgement to appease them. As a result, my ship and crew were captured by the authorities in a place not of my choosing. The humiliation was mine. The responsibility of defense became mine. Most of the crew refused to participate in raising funds for the defense or doing any work for the defense. They fell back to the position of not taking responsibility. The lesson that I learned then was that decisions can only be made by those who have their head on the block. Responsibility for consequences contributes to correct decision-making in the field.

FIELD CONFRONTATION

*Vi et Armis **

This chapter is for environmental actions that take place in the field. It is meant for those actions which take place in wilderness terrain or urban jungles.

Always exercise forethought and never make light of your opponent.

Camp in high places facing the sun. Make sure that you command the view of your terrain. When spiking trees, always start at the top of the terrain and work down. Always post guards and work out a code of signals.

Do not initiate a confrontation with your back to a river or body of water. After crossing a river, move quickly away from it. If you must engage your opponent on a river, always approach from upstream. Never move upstream to engage. Never anchor below your enemy.

Never put yourself in a position with your back facing cliffs, swift flowing streams, confined places, tangled thickets, or any other natural hazard. Always give yourself room to retreat.

Within the neighbourhood of your camp, survey and routinely inspect surrounding hills, hollows, ponds, thick grass, bushes, and trees. These are locations where the enemy may lie in ambush or spy upon your movements.

When your enemy is close at hand and quiet, they are relying on the natural strength of their position. When the enemy tries to provoke a confrontation, they are anxious for you to advance. If the encampment of the enemy is easy to approach, beware of a possible trap.

Look for the sudden rising of birds in flight to alert you to the movement of people. Startled wild animals are the best sign of an approaching opposition.

If birds gather on any spot, it is a sign that the area is free of people.

Pay close attention to the signs of nature. Disturbances can easily be

Latin: Vi et armis means "by force of arms."

detected. The approach of humans can easily be detected. Study and look for these signs.

In urban areas, do not attract attention to yourself by running from an incident. Blend in with the people on the street. Do not appear nervous.

In the wilderness, if the enemy approaches loudly, assume confidence among their ranks. If the enemy is quiet, assume lack of confidence or stealth among their ranks.

To avoid pursuit, do not run. At the first opportunity, find a means to blend in. That which is obvious is sometimes less suspect.

> Once while on board a ship that I was sabotaging, I attracted the attention of the police because of my use of a flashlight. They had seen the flicker from the road. Instead of hiding on board the ship, I immediately went on deck and surprised the two police officers who were just getting out of their car on the dock. I greeted them cordially. One officer apologized saying he did not know that the ship had crew on board. He told me that he thought that I was a robber. I thanked him for his concern and told him that I had just arrived and that I was attempting to get a generator working. The police left. I started the generator and completed my work with the benefit of the light and electricity.

Always plan your avenues of escape. Know the terrain. It is also good to have a cover, false identification, and an alibi.

TERRAIN AND SITUATION

A Fronte Paecipitium A Tergo Lupi *

Terrain and situations can be categorized as accessible, entrapping, indecisive, constricted, high, and distant.

Terrain and situations which can be crossed freely and with little difficulty is called accessible. The advantage lies with the side that can most quickly take up a position on such terrain or seize the first advantage of a situation. The advantage lies with the party that moves most swiftly. On open ground, monkey-wrenchers, survey stake removers, hunt saboteurs, and others must move quickly and in a disciplined manner.

Some terrain and some situations are easy to get out of but difficult to return to. The nature of this position is that the advantage is only yours IF the enemy is unprepared. If your enemy is prepared and you do not win, it will be difficult to withdraw. This type of situation is entanglement and the terrain is entrapping. This is not a good situation.

> In 1986, David Howitt and Rod Coronado successfully scuttledhalf of Iceland's whaling fleet. This tactic worked in Iceland because the Icelanders were not prepared. The tactic would not have worked in Japan where the whalers are prepared for sabotage.

Terrain or situations that are equally disadvantageous to both sides are called indecisive. The enemy will attempt to offer bait to entice you out onto the disadvantaged ground. Do not go forth. Withdraw and feign weakness. Draw out the other side into the weak position then turn and strike swiftly and decisively. Do not allow your opposition to choose your targets for you. In British Columbia, the logging companies deliberately announce plans to log

* Latin: A fronte praecipitium a tergo lupi means literally, "a precipice in front, wolves behind." A more modern meaning would be "between a rock and a hard place."

pristine and environmentally sensitive areas. Such an announcement is then followed by a predictable response. As a result, energy and resources are expended in the direction chosen by the logging companies. Other less pristine and ecologically sensitive areas are ignored by the environmental groups and can then be logged without opposition. In British Columbia, the logging companies have been implementing a superior strategy. The environmental movement has simply responded to the strategy of the opposition and thus the environmental movement has been channelled and controlled by the logging interests.

On constricted ground like a narrow pass, you can only use this type of terrain if you arrive and survey, fortify, and control the position first. You can then await the opposition. Never pursue or seek out the enemy after your enemy has taken possession of restricted terrain before you. When spiking trees in a mountainous region, you must deploy observers with radios on the roads leading into and out of the area. With the observers in place, tree-spiking can proceed without fear of discovery. If the opposition approaches, all activity ceases and the tree-spikers can remain hidden in the woods. Be prepared to spend time in the forest. Never leave a vehicle in the area. All activists must be dropped off and retrieved at a pre-determined time. You must control the access points to the area to be effective.

The same rule applies to high ground. Arrive first and you can hold it. Never assault a force occupying a position of height. When camping near a body of water, always stake your tent and supplies on high ground.

With regard to distant ground, your supply lines must be strong and protected. It is important to have capable leaders and followers who can exploit both natural resources and the supplies of the enemy.

When followers are too strong and the leaders are too weak, the result is insubordination.

When the leaders are too strong and the followers too weak, the result is collapse or chaos.

When officers are angry and insubordinate to the leader, the result is ruin.

When a leader is weak and has no authority; when orders are not clear and distinct; when there are no fixed duties assigned to officers and followers, the result will be disorganization.

When a leader is unable to survey the enemy's strength and sends an inferior force to engage a superior force, the result will be destruction of one's followers.

These are the six guarantees of defeat: neglect to estimate the strength of the enemy, lack of authority, insufficient training, unjustified anger, lack of discipline, and the failure to select trained and disciplined followers.

If the leader knows the terrain and can estimate the opposition, can control the forces, and calculate difficulties, distance, and dangers, there will be triumph. If not, there will be defeat.

If you know the enemy and know yourself, you will not be endangered. If you know the ground, control the situation, and know the weather, you will be victorious.

Decisions of strategy in the field must be made in the field. Decisions in the field cannot be made by bureaucrats who are removed from the situation.

A leader must be unconcerned with fame or material gain. A decision to advance or retreat cannot be made properly unless independent of the desires of the leader. The only desire of the leader that must be cultivated is the desire to triumph over the opposition and to attain objectives.

Leaders must respect their followers.

The environmental movement must respect the terrain of grassroots environmental groups. Large national groups will foment animosity by initiating campaigns without coordination with local groups.

Grassroot groups are the strength of the ecology movement.

Two or more grassroots groups in the same area with similar objectives but with different tactics must agree to disagree on tactical approaches. If they do not then energies will be expended on unproductive dispute over non-objective issues. The opposition will win because our forces have been divided.

If one group does not like another group then it should adopt a policy of mutual non-criticism. If one group does not refrain from criticizing, the group that does refrain will be morally superior and must hold fast to a policy of non-retaliation.

In some situations, it is advantageous for a grassoots group to publicly criticize a large national or international organization on the grounds of bureaucracy, abuse of funds, exploitation of issues, and corruption.

Many large, environmental organizations are reflections of the system. In some cases, the difference in morality, organization, bureaucracy, and self-interest between multinational corporations and multinational environmental organizations are practically indistinguishable.

When an environmental group operates for profit and is insensitive to grassroots organizations, such an ecocorporation should be criticized.

It rarely profits a large environmental group to criticize a smaller grassroots group.

Sometimes the opposition will set up a grassroots group in an attempt to co-opt an issue. If this is done, the connections should be investigated and exposed with credibility.

An Earth Warrior must be aware of terrain and situations. The warrior must be able to survey, occupy, secure, or decline to hold a location or situation.

The warrior must be able to control both the situation and all directions of the terrain.

THE NINE SITUATIONS
Tu ne cede malis sed contra audentior ito *

In the area of environmental confrontation there are nine situations.

The first is the situation of being a local hero. This means you are a member of a community tackling an outside force intent upon damaging your community's ecosystem. The more respected you are within your community, the more powerful your position will be.

In this situation you have a moral advantage. The outside force will attack with economic promise. The prospect of employment opportunities is a strong motivation for winning over support from a community. Many people are, however, reluctant to alienate themselves from their own community. The stronger the community spirit in opposition to the offerings of the enemy, the less motivation there will be for those seeking employment from the opposition.

A community leader in this situation should seek to control the local media. If unwilling, the local media can be influenced by seeking to influence local advertisers who are in an even better situation to influence the media.

Parents can be influenced by their children so it is important that you seek to educate children in your community about environmental dangers.

Seek the support of local law enforcement people. Win them to your side. If forced to choose between you and outside forces, they should side with you.

Seek to transform your opposition into an environmentally negative force of outsiders. Bring the community together as a positive force which opposes these detrimental, outside interests. Them versus Us.

Do not openly humiliate or ridicule those in your community who side with the enemy. Be patient with them. Be friendly to them. At every opportunity you must gently inform them of the dangers to the community, of the dangers to their children, and to those they love.

* Latin: Tu ne cede malis sed contra audentior ito means "yield not to misfortunes, but advance all the more boldly against them." A quotation from Virgil's *Aeneid*.

Always seek to turn your fellow citizen against an Earth destroying employer.

Keep the attack focused on the polluter.

The second situation is that of the outside agitator. In this situation the circumstances are the reverse of the first. You are now the outsider. The enemy is either moving into the community or is already entrenched.

In this situation, do not expect to win friends if the enemy has already secured inside loyalty. If the enemy has not, seek to recruit allies who will then carry the torch. The leaders of the cause should be local citizens. Your position should be as advisor.

An incomplete strategy can backfire.

As an example, I reported on a community in Washington State in 1974 where a nuclear reactor was being built. I was representing a newspaper and decided to take an objective look at the situation. In my role, I did not condone nor condemn nuclear power. I found that most of the residents of Elma, Washington were against the reactor.

After my report, there was a demonstration that took place sponsored by an anti-nuclear group from Seattle. The demonstrators talked down to the local residents. They insinuated that the locals were stupid for allowing the reactor to be built. One sign said, "If you cared for your children Elma, you would not tolerate nuclear power."

As the residents watched gay groups, feminist groups, and socialists groups all parade by tacking personal agendas to the nuclear issue, they became angry. As a result, my interviews the day after the demonstration revealed that the town was much more sympathetic to the nuclear power people.

One resident said to me, "At least them nuclear people are Americans."

If the community is firmly against you then utilize the strategy of embarrassing the community by appealing to a larger community. Turn the outside media upon them.

> In 1984, I travelled with a crew to the north of British Columbia to challenge a government-sponsored wolf hunt. The community of Fort Nelson was firmly in favor of the hunt and quite hostile to us.
>
> I called a town meeting. The provincial and national media had followed us to the North.
>
> With the cameras rolling, I met their collective hostility with indignation. I fed their hatred of me and our cause with inflammatory statements.
>
> Two rednecks came storming in and threw the bodies of two wolves down on the floor at my feet.
>
> "What do ya think of that, asshole?" they shouted at me.
>
> "I think you just lost this round," I answered.
>
> As a result, the outside news coverage was emotionally weighed against my opposition. The next day, one Toronto newspaper called the town "Fort Neanderthal".
>
> The town of Fort Nelson was thus nationally humiliated within the context of their larger community. This caused many residents to reconsider the position they were promoting in light of public condemnation from fellow Canadians.

It is important to be aware of your situation. Are you coming from within or from without? Each requires a different strategy.

The third situation is the legal high ground. This situation means that you have the support of law. These laws may be municipal, state, or national. The laws in this situation are the laws of the community where the confrontation takes place.

It is important in this situation to act within the context of the law. Use the law to strike your opposition. Use lawyers and utilize the legal system.

Respect the laws as tactics even if you do not respect the laws philosophically.

Seek to represent other species or habitat in the courts. If standing is granted, then make use of it. If standing is not granted, then fight through the courts to gain the right for standing.

> In 1984, the group Friends of the Wolf were denied standing in the Province of British Columbia to defend wolves by challenging the legal right of the Provincial government to kill them. The group persisted. In 1988, Friends of the Wolf, in an alliance with the Western Canada Wilderness Committee, succeeded in obtaining standing and succeeded in legally shutting down the wolf hunt.

The fourth situation is to strike illegally but visibly. This is called civil disobedience. When utilizing this tactic, you must remain faithful to the principle of non-violence. Civil disobedience is a non-violent tactic.

You must be prepared for the moral and legal consequences for your actions. Make preparations for bail or for possible fines. Make preparations for retaining a lawyer or prepare to defend yourself.

Never forget the just nature of your cause.

Sometimes to challenge the validity of a law you must break the law in order to do so.

> In 1983, I took my ship and crew into Canadian waters to challenge the Canadian Seal Protection Act. This Act was an Orwellian set of regulations designed ostensibly for seal protection, but in reality was implemented to protect the sealing industry. It was an unjust law.
>
> We deliberately and flagrantly broke these laws and we were arrested and put on trial.
>
> The courts were hostile and we were convicted. We appealed to the higher court and we were acquitted. The government appealed our acquittal and we won.

The Supreme Court of Canada then ruled that the Seal Protection Act was unconstitutional.

We challenged the law by breaking it and in the process we defeated the law and had it removed.

Civil Disobedience requires that people have the courage to stand by their convictions, you must have faith in your cause.

The fifth situation is to operate under the authority of international rules, regulations, laws, and treaties. This situation is primarily for confrontations in international waters where there is no law enforcement body with the powers of jurisdiction.

Most of my activities with Sea Shepherd confrontation utilize the fifth situation. Sea Shepherd campaigns utilize existing treaties or regulations to justify actions against those who are illegally killing whales, seals, dolphins, birds, turtles, or fish, or who are damaging habitat.

In 1979, when I rammed the pirate whaler, *Sierra*, the owners of the outlaw whaler could not charge me without admitting to ownership, which would have caused serious political and financial repercussions to them.

In 1986, when David Howitt and Rod Coronado sank half of Iceland's whaling fleet, the Icelandic government refused to lay charges in fear of the embarrassment that would have been caused by international exposure of their illegal whaling activities.

In 1990, when I rammed and disabled two Japanese drift net vessels in the mid-Pacific, the government of Japan and the Japanese fishing industry refused to acknowledge that the action had even taken place for fear of increasing the negative exposure of their drift net operations.

Utilizing the fifth situation is a form of setting yourself up as an unofficial law enforcement agency. You are, in fact, taking vigilante action. However, the failure of enforcement of laws against those you oppose due to the nonexistence of an official enforcement agency will enable you to likewise remain free to do as you wish. If you could be stopped, then so should your opposition. If your opposition is free to do what they wish, then so are you. All that is then important is to possess a superior strategy than your opposition.

The sixth situation is infiltration. This means that you seek to join and rise in the ranks of your opposition. You will then be in a position to damage or control your opposition.

The sixth situation requires much preparation and discipline. It is highly effective. I could give examples of this situation working, but to do so would be to blow the covers of the infiltrators, all of whom continue to be effective.

Targets for using the sixth situation include government, business, other more established environmental organizations, schools, and the media.

The seventh situation is exposure. In this situation, you must build up a public image which places you in the limelight at all times. To do this you must achieve celebrity status. Better yet, you should build your image into a legend. Become notoriously famous. Fame is a weapon and it is a weapon that can be used both defensively and offensively.

If not personally famous, then enlist the aid of the famous in your cause. The recruitment of celebrities is a legitimate tactic.

Many environmental causes have been and are being championed by celebrities.

> In 1977, I took Brigitte Bardot to the ice fields off Labrador. The photograph of her posing cheek to cheek with a baby seal pup made the cover of *Paris Match* and numerous European magazines and directly influenced the decision of the European Common Market to ban seal pelts from Canada.

The eighth situation is that of wealth. Money can influence many situations and further many causes. The rich can be powerful allies. If one cultivates wealth for the purpose of fomenting positive ecological causes, it is a noble thing. Money is a weapon and a tool. Money is a force that can be directed positively when controlled with an intelligent strategy.

Money can be used to buy and protect land.

Money can be used to fund research, educational campaigns, or for direct action.

Fund-raising is an essential component of any movement. The ability to raise funds is a valuable skill. Knowledge of finance and economics is a valuable skill. An Earth warrior can wield a checkbook with more clout than a sword or a gun.

The ninth and final situation is the covert strategy. This situation is the most dangerous and desperate situation of all.

The ninth situation requires striking both illegally and sometimes with great destruction.

The first rule here is: DO NOT GET CAUGHT!

Being arrested will tie up both your time and your resources. You will then become effectively monitored and controlled by the State. Your movements will be limited and your freedom will be restricted. If you go to jail you will be removed from the fight for a brief or a prolonged time, perhaps for life. The consequences for getting caught in covert activities are not insignificant.

The second rule for covert activities is: DO NOT KILL OR INJURE ANY LIVING THING!

To cause a death or an injury is contradictory to the tenet of the Earth Warrior that life is to be respected. Additionally, a death or an injury to the opposition may result in a political and moral backlash against you and the cause you represent.

The third rule for covert activities is: DO NOT GET YOURSELF OR YOUR FOLLOWERS AND ALLIES KILLED OR INJURED.

You or your followers will be of little use to the Earth if hospitalized, maimed, or in a grave.

An exception to this rule can be made if you are suffering from a terminal disease. If the expenditure of your life will bring about a positive development for the Ecosystem, then such a death is more noble and satisfying then a lingering painful demise in a hospital bed with tubes running through your bodily orifices.

A human being should live with nobility and die with nobility.

With reference to Rule One: Do Not Get Caught.

To ensure that you do not get caught, follow this advice:

1. Carry out covert actions alone. Do not write down any plans or ideas. Do not speak of your plans in advance. Do not speak of your actions afterwards. No person, and I mean NO PERSON WITHOUT EXCEPTION, need ever know of your activities. Ego gratification is not sufficient reason to be caught, fined, jailed, or worse. Protect yourself by shutting up.

2. If you must work with other people do so following this advice:

First Choice: Work only with close, blood relatives—brother, sister, son, daughter, father, mother, grandfather, grandmother, grandchildren—BUT only if you intuitively and ideologically trust them. Make sure that they share your views and agree with your tactics. Even so, there is a real risk working covertly and illegally with any person other than yourself.

Second Choice: Comrades and friends, but ONLY if you have known the individual or individuals for at least seven years. Make no exceptions. Seven years is a long time for a representative of the enemy to invest in infiltration. Even so, there is a real risk working covertly and illegally with any other person.

NEVER become involved in a covert illegal activity with your lover, (i.e., girlfriend, boyfriend, wife, or husband.) The relationship between lovers is the most unstable relationship of all. You could be betrayed to the authorities because of an emotional rift resulting from jealousy or spite. The partner may later regret doing so but by then it will be too late. If you decide to make an exception here because you feel that your relationship is "different," then you must analyze the situation and proceed with the knowledge of your risk— which is considerable.

Have absolutely nothing to do with any person who approaches you with a plan of covert or direct action unless you have known them for seven years.

Always maintain a healthy paranoia about people. Temper your paranoia with observation, common sense, and learn to trust in your intuition.

Never discuss an action, a strategy, or tactics on the telephone or inside a house. Always undertake discussions of this nature outside in the open, under the sky, and always vary the location.

Never take notes about an action. If you must write down directions, destroy them without trace immediately after use.

Photocopy machines can be traced. Avoid them when sending communiques unless you use a public machine some distance from where you reside or work. Always check to ensure you did not leave the original in the machine before you leave. Avoid typewriters and data processors in the same way. Never hand write a communique. Never leave information of a sensitive nature in your computer's memory or on diskettes. Do not send sensitive information through the mail unless you are sending it to the authorities or the media. Then always mail from a location far from where you live. Do not send any sensitive information or communiques by fax machine.

When communicating, use code and change it frequently.

Always keep covert actions simple.

Always wear gloves and cover your hair to prevent hair loss. Leave nothing at the site you attack unless you leave it intentionally.

If arrested, remember this advice: the authorities are not your friends. They are out to screw you, to put you away, to mess you up. Do not talk with them, joke with them, or antagonize them. Be courteous but do not engage in small talk.

Remember this slogan: NOBODY TALKS—EVERYBODY WALKS.

Ignore threats. Ignore kind words. Ignore accusations that your friends have already talked so you may as well come clean. Chances are they have not, especially if you selected your accomplices correctly—especially if you have agreed in advance that NOBODY TALKS.

Chances are that the only evidence they have is your words. Chances are that if you all keep quiet, you will all walk out the door free.

Always assume that your accomplices have NOT talked. Never take the word of an enemy representative on anything .

Also, remember that you must never sign anything unless you have been advised by a lawyer.

A good slogan here is: NOBODY SIGNS—EVERYTHING'S FINE.

Another strategy to utilize is the Brer Rabbit ploy. If you have a political or moral advantage then let the authorities know and believe that you want to be put on trial.

> In January 1988, I flew to Iceland to demand that the Icelandic authorities charge me for the sinking of half of Iceland's whaling fleet which we had sunk in 1986.
>
> I told the authorities that they should charge me and that I was at their mercy to decide what should be done with me.
>
> This action resulted in a debate in the Icelandic parliament where an Icelandic member of Parliament stated that they would not play into my hands by doing what I wanted to do. As a result, I was deported without charge and Iceland was publicly and internationally embarrassed.

If the system does manage to get you into court there are many strategies that can be utilized.

Captain John Cormack, when he skippered the *Greenpeace V,* once told me:

"NEVER ADMIT NUTHIN"

In court, never volunteer information. Use a minimum of words to answer any question put to you. Never perjure yourself by lying, but never tell the truth if the truth is going to contribute towards your conviction. You do not have to lie. Avoid the truth, evade the truth, twist the truth.

Employ the Ronald Reagan strategy for maintaining a minimum of information output:

I CAN'T REMEMBER.

I CAN'T RECALL.

I HAVE NO RECOLLECTIONS OF THOSE EVENTS.

I'M NOT SURE.

I WASN'T AWARE OF ANY WRONG DOING.

Never make a fuss about swearing on the bible. It's only a book and you do not want to prejudice your case by directly insulting or alienating the anthropocentric Christians or Jews. It is their book and you are in their power. When in Rome let them believe that you're as devoutly anthropocentric as they are, maybe even more so.

Deception can save your ass in this situation.

Go into court clean-cut, well mannered and be polite, friendly, and all-American or all- whatever. You're on their territory. Skilled deception is required. Utilize the Ollie North strategy. Dress more establishment than the prosecutor or the lawyers. Keep your attire conservative, but not too expensive. Take on the demeanor of a boy or girl scout. If you are qualified or if you can get away with it, then wear a uniform.

Always address the judge politely as "your Honor." Always refer to the prosecutor as "this honorable gentleman or gentlewoman." Always say "yes" or "yes sir/yes madam." Never say "ya" or "sure." Never use slang. Demonstrate that you are intelligent, educated, cool tempered—the very opposite of a fanatic anything. Demonstrate emotional concern for the Earth and for people. Do not be overly emotional.

Appeal to the emotions of the jury. Do not be cold, aloof, or arrogant. If there is a jury, they must be influenced to like you. The judge should be influenced to respect you. Never be antagonistic. Remember that you are the David and you are facing the Goliath.

In court your weapons are your lawyer, your credibility, your humility, and your presentability. Cultivate charisma and arm yourself with it. Cloak yourself in charm and graciousness. Be a gentle person. Most importantly - never forget that you are right, that your actions are justified, and that your intent is honorable.

In 1971, I was on trial in Vancouver, B.C. on charges of willful damage to property. A takeover of property that I had helped to organize to prevent construction of a hotel, had resulted in the complete destruction of a wooden fence surrounding the site. I was given a trial by judge and jury. During my testimony I talked about protecting the site of nesting Canada geese. I appealed directly to the jury, to their love of nature, to their patriotic duty to protect the land.

The opposition talked only of money and of the loss of profit to their share-holders. The jury deliberated the charges for only three minutes before acquitting me.

These are the nine situations.

THE CODE OF THE ECO-WARRIOR

"Rule Number One: Don't get caught.
Rule Number Two: Don't get caught.
Rule Number Three: If you do get caught you're on your own. Nobody goes your bail. Nobody hires you a lawyer. Nobody pays your fines."

- George Washington Hayduke
from Hayduke Lives!

ATTACKING WITH FIRE

Similia similibus curantur *

Sun Tzu recommends five areas that fire may be employed. The first area is to burn personnel. This is not a method recommended by this book. An Earth Warrior must refrain from deliberately attempting to take life.

Of the remaining four areas: the first is to burn supplies, the second is to burn equipment, the third is to burn weapons, and the fourth is the use of explosives and missiles.

When using fire as a tool, always factor in the strength and direction of the wind, and the dryness of the target area. Many fire attacks depend on the weather.

When wind blows during the day, it will die down at night.

When using fire to attack, always approach the enemy from downwind.

Always prepare your materials in advance and research your materials so as to apply to your needs.

If you burn the enemy supplies in the field, it will damage the opposition.

It is most effective to use fire to destroy weapons and equipment.

Fire can be effectively used as a distraction.

There are two types of fire: Controlled and uncontrolled.

Fires can be controlled in the form of oxygen and acetylene bottles and this method is ideal for attacks on machinery or stationery metal targets such as billboards or bulldozers. Underwater cutting torches can sink ships.

Gasoline or explosive fires are uncontrollable. Once set into motion, these materials cannot be stopped without extensive damage. The possibility of causing death or injury is a serious consideration.

Never utilize explosives without proper instructions in the use of these weapons.

Explosives and fire are unpredictable. Exercise extreme caution.

* Latin: Similia Similibus curantur literally means, "like things are cured by likes" or "fight fire with fire."

The use of fire is meant for situations which demand a radical attack. Fire means maximum damage.

The use of fire will provoke anger in your opposition. Be prepared for this anger.

The use of fire is not advisable in overt operations. Fire and explosives are difficult to justify from a public relations point of view. Arson is a serious crime.

Fire and explosives are most effectively used in covert operations.

If fire is used against you. Do not panic. Read the direction of the fire, stay low to the ground, and retreat.

Explosives can be used against you. Always check your vehicle for evidence of tampering before you engage the ignition. Use smoke detectors and fire extinguishers. Be prepared for attack by fire or explosives.

Always use fire to dispose of papers and materials that may be used as evidence against you. Always scatter the ashes.

Learn how to make a fire in the field. It could save your life.

Fire is effective, extreme, unpredictable, and dangerous. Be well versed in utilizing fire for offensive strategies and be prepared to deal with fire from a defensive stance.

Chemicals may be used tactically in some cases.

There are chemicals which cause extreme odors that are effective for vacating areas or for crowd dispersal. Pay attention to the direction of the wind if used in the open. Allow for orderly escape if used in enclosed areas.

Smoke may be utilized for the same purpose or for masking an approach.

Chemical acids may be used to damage machinery.

When attacking chemical plants or facilities, be familiar with the degree of toxicity of the chemicals on the site. Have a protective suit available if there is a danger of a spill.

Our established culture has developed a chemically intensive society. There are over 100,000 different manufactured chemicals in production. The chemical companies are in the front lines of those we oppose.

To combat the chemical armada, we must understand and we must employ chemistry. Fire can be fought with fire. Chemicals can be fought with chemicals or the knowledge of chemistry.

If you utilize explosives, it is advisable that you have training, either military or industrial. Lack of knowledge may kill you and others.

To kill with explosives intentionally is cowardly and can seldom be justified within the strategy of a warrior serving the Earth. However if it is the only defense available, it should be carefully prepared and executed with extreme efficiency.

Fire, explosives, and chemicals should be used tactically only by experts.

Fire as a strategy means total destruction of the supplies and equipment of your opposition. In our society, the most vulnerable targets are computers. Strike destructively at the data base of your enemy and you will succeed in inflicting heavy losses. Power and information are one and the same in a media defined culture.

Remember, it is a weak strategy that includes poorly prepared tactics

"It seems to be a law inflexible and inexorable
that he who will not risk cannot win."
John Paul Jones

⑬

THE USE OF INTELLIGENCE AGENTS

Nam Et Ipsa Scientia Potestas Est *

The most cost effective method of defeating an opposition is through the intelligent use of intelligence agents.

Agents cost much less than fielding an expeditionary force in the field.

In confronting your opposition, spare no expense in using agents to investigate the enemy situation.

Success against your opposition depends heavily on foreknowledge of opposition movements and opposition strategies.

The only way of gaining foreknowledge is to infiltrate the opposition with agents. Your agents must be able to discover, to know, and to relay the enemy position to you.

There are five types of agents that can be utilized. These five are native, inside, doubled, expendable, and living agents.

If you can arrange an intelligence structure utilizing all five types of agents, then you will have the ideal arrangement for an effective intelligence at your service .

Native agents are citizens employed from the enemy country.

Inside agents are employees of your opposition who work for you.

Doubled agents are enemy spies that you employ.

Expendable agents are those of your employ who are deliberately given fabricated information.

Living agents are those that are able to return with valuable information.

Native or Local Agents

It is wise to recruit citizens of enemy nations to relay information to you. Citizens can be convinced to do so by appealing to their ideological motives

---

* Latin: Nam et ipsa scientia potestas est means "knowledge is power."

(the most effective), or through financial incentive, or coercion.

Provide your native agents with funds and praise. Provide them with their requests. These are valuable agents. They speak the language and they can move about with more freedom than non-native agents.

Always be prepared for betrayal by a native agent.

> I *cannot* give specific examples of my own use of native agents without betraying the confidentiality of my past and present agents. Suffice to say, in every campaign, I have utilized local people for the following purposes:
>
> 1. To prepare reports on terrain, movements of ships and cargoes, locations, relevant individuals, and relevant information.
> 2. To distribute both information and disinformation.
> 3. To cause diversions.
> 4. To provide cover, shelter, and supplies.
> 5. To translate relevant information.
> 6. To infiltrate for information and/or sabotage.

Inside or Internal Agents

Inside any organization or government you will find dissatisfied officials. Many of these officials can be enlisted to your cause by appealing to their ideals and desires. Although not completely trustworthy, these agents can provide much valuable information.

A more reliable inside agent is one of your own, one you have trained to infiltrate the enemy ranks.

Reward these people generously.

> One of our female agents, dressed seductively, arranged a meeting in Norway with a whaling company official. Presenting one of her false business cards, she introduced herself as a buyer for a major Japanese seafood company. She

negotiated a sale with the whaling company for four tons of whale meat. She carried with her a falsified letter of credit from a Japanese bank and details for shipping. Cash on delivery.

The whale meat was shipped to Panama for trans-shipment to Japan. Our agent then notified another agent who met the shipment in Panama, and he was able to bribe longshoremen to give him access to the containers holding the whale meat. He disconnected the freezers and jammed the temperature gauges to indicated nothing was wrong.

The meat arrived in Japan in a less than fresh state. The Japanese were not aware that it was arriving. The Norwegians were, to say the least, extremely angry and, most importantly, the operation cost the whaling company a great deal of money.

Double or Converted Agents

When you discover enemy agents working against you, offer to recruit them. Reward them generously. Keep them reporting minor or false information to their other employers. Watch them carefully.

The best use of these agents is to convey false information to the opposition.

On four occasions, I have had government agents infiltrate my crew. On two occasions, I was able to suspect their role and thus I was able to exploit their skills, keep an eye on them, and prevent any damage or leak in plans.

On two other occasions, one agent was caught attempting to sabotage the engine and another agent was able to damage the engine and delay a campaign.

Because of these incidents, I suspect all members of the crew and watch them closely until I can determine to my satisfaction that they can be trusted.

The Greenpeace Foundation in New Zealand was successfully infiltrated by a French government agent. As a result, the Greenpeace flagship, the *Rainbow Warrior,* was mined and sunk.

Earth First! was successfully infiltrated by agents of the Federal Bureau of Investigation in the United States. As a result, some Earth First! activists were set up, arrested, and jailed.

Expendable Agents

An expendable agent is one of your own people that you send on a mission for one of two purposes:

1. A suicide mission with no or little possibility of escape.

2. An agent who is given false or fabricated information so that they will be deliberately caught, and the information will be made available to the opposition in a credible manner.

Expendable agents must not have knowledge of their real role. They too must be deceived.

Expendable agents must not be of much value. They are to be sacrificed as part of a tactical procedure.

On the first day of January, 1980, I was forced to scuttle one of my own ships in the Port of Leixoes in Portugal. I had taken a crew into Portugal a few days earlier to steal my ship back from Portuguese officials who had taken custody of it in retribution for scuttling the *Sierra.*

One of my crew was an infiltrator from an environmental organization that was attempting to sabotage us.

Upon arriving, we found the ship both looted and disabled.

I informed the infiltrator that we would scuttle the ship and head north, each of us separately. After scuttling the ship, my crew and I went to the south. The infiltrator headed north, and because we had left numerous signs of heading north, the infiltrator was apprehended and immediately told the officials that we were all heading north to meet in Spain.

This bought us time to reach the south and cross the border into Spain. We escaped.

The infiltrator spent four weeks in a Portuguese jail and then was released.

Living Agents

These agents are the men and women who form the backbone of your intelligence operation. They should be people of intelligence, but give a foolish or common appearance. They must be strong-willed, active, healthy, physically strong, and courageous. They must be accustomed to dirty work, able to endure hunger and cold, heat, and exposure. They must be able to tolerate humiliation.

Your intelligence agents should be familiars. They should be praised and they should be liberally rewarded.

The most important discipline to insist upon of your agents is one of secrecy. They must be able to keep their mouths shut.

In choosing an agent, you must look for integrity of character, skills, and experience.

Agents must be managed with benevolence and straight-forwardness.

It is imperative that a leader have a subtle ingenuity in order to ascertain the truthfulness of their agent's reports.

Always be subtle.

Utilize your agents often in all your affairs.

A breach in secrecy must be punished severely.

Always be vigilant for enemy agents.

Converted agents can be used to recruit native and internal agents.

The information acquired from the native and internal agents can be used for setting up an expendable agent.

All this information acquired by the first four types of spies can be used by the living agent.

The purpose of intelligence agents is to acquire knowledge of the opposition. This knowledge can be best obtained from the converted or double agent. This agent brings information and makes it possible for the others to operate to an advantage. Thus, the converted agent should always be treated with respect.

Intelligence is the most important element of any conflict.

THE 36 STRATEGIES

Miyamoto Musashi laid the recklessness of his youth upon the anvil of disciplined study. Before he was able to unsheathe the sword of expertise, he had to first unfurl the scrolls of wisdom and dedicate himself to the study of strategy. One of these scrolls, of ancient Chinese origin, was imperative for focusing the young Musashi on building his foundation for strategy. The author is today unknown. Most certainly the anonymous sage was influenced by Sun Tzu. The study was and is simply known as the "Thirty Six Strategies."

I have taken the liberty of translating these strategies into workable formulas for the ecologist activist.

These strategies are:

1. The Art of Invisibility. This is the creation of a situation that, through time, becomes familiar or the creation of a situation that gives an impression of familiarity. Within this situation the strategist may move and maneuver unseen. This means that the activist must blend into the community. The activist must cultivate a routine that trains all observers that there is nothing unusual about his or her movements. This is the art of not attracting attention. It was by this means that the legendary Fox was able to gain access to the head offices of Standard Oil in Chicago. He looked like a painter and his apparent task was to paint the president's office. He proceeded to do so during lunch hour, painting the office with foul-smelling oil and the carcasses of dead birds, fish and frogs.

2. The Helpful Big Brother Scheme. When a weak organization is being challenged by a stronger group, a third organization can come to the defense of the weaker organization thus gaining trust and loyalty and eventually absorbing the defended group without risk of open hostility. At the same time the aggressor organization can be weakened and given a bad reputation for aggression. Defender gains benevolent control evolving into complete control. David McTaggart utilized this scheme when he mediated a dispute between Greenpeace Canada and Greenpeace USA in 1979. He emerged as International Chairman of Greenpeace International with absolute authority.

3. The Virtue of Friends. If your organization is weakened, appeal to friends and allies for assistance. If you are weakened as an individual, appeal to your friends. Have your friends and allies bear the brunt of conflict while you gather and replenish your strength. Bear in mind that you have many types of friends and allies. Use your "expendable friends" first and foremost, your valued friends only as a last resort. Reward their contributions generously and cultivate their future possibilities.

4. Be Rested as Your Opponent Wearies. Always force your opposition to expend energy while you maintain your own. Before conflict, you must weary your opponent with diversionary tactics and false alarms that cost you little in resources or energy. Have your opponent come to you. Force your opposition to expend resources without achieving results. Observe and monitor and when your opposition is sufficiently weakened—strike!

5. As Others Drown, Dive for the Pearl. Always use the troubles of others as an opportunity to gain for your cause. As others panic, keep calm and observe the environment for an opportunity to advance. The calm warrior steps adroitly around the burning wreckage, selects what is needed and escapes unseen and undetected.

6. Spreading Manure. Give out false information about your intentions and movements. Leave false clues and signals. Lead your opposition to concentrate defense and offense on fronts more desirable for your advantage. When you say that you will be doing one thing, then do another. If utilized often as a strategy, counter sometimes by doing exactly what you suggest when it is apparent that your opponent believes that you are bluffing.

7. Materializing the Ghost. Create a fantasy before the eyes of your opponent and leave clues and suggestions that will lead your opponent to believe your fantasy is reality. Suggest to your opponent that you have what you do not, that you are stronger than you are. By this means you can create security with little expenditure.

8. The Wizard of Oz. A false front. The illusion of a center of strength. A lightning rod for the concerns of your opposition. Have your opponent concentrate on your center of apparent strength as you attack from the mists and the darkness.

9. The Strategy of Passive Observation. Watch your opponents and if they engage in conflict, observe and do not interfere. Stand ready to walk through the ashes to retrieve what can be salvaged.

10. Cloak and Dagger. Infiltrate your opposition. Gain their trust. Win their confidence. When you have the complete trust of your opponents, you can then move secretly against them. Sam LaBudde used this strategy when he crewed on board a Panamanian tuna seiner for the purpose of documenting the killing of dolphins.

11. The Strategy of Sacrifice. The strategist must be prepared to make individual sacrifices to achieve a greater objective. Leadership of a campaign, a crusade or an organization requires sacrifice on the part of the leader. The objectives must take precedence over all other considerations including personal concerns.

12. The Strategy of Resourcefulness. A strategist must take advantage of any and all opportunities. Utilize available materials and resources and seek to be aware of what is available for your advantage. When operating covertly, always appear calm and behave naturally.

13. Piercing the Veil. When your opponent is hidden and the strategy of your opposition is unknown, the Warrior must initiate an action designed to bait a response. Test your opposition and observe both tactical strength and strategic wisdom.

14. The Strategy of Innovation and Imagination. Do not do what others do. Do not duplicate the strategies of others. Use new tactics and resurrect tactics that have been forgotten. The tactic of treespiking, which was used by the Industrial Workers of the World in the early 20th century, was later used as an environmental tactic to protect trees in the latter part of the century.

You must constantly escalate and change your strategy especially in a media culture where what is exciting today is old news tomorrow. For example, ramming a whaling ship was big news when I did it in 1979 but not good enough a few years later. We then had to sink a whaler. A few years after that, we had to sink half a whaling fleet. The media culture especially demands innovation and imagination, and always with an eye for visuals and a flair for the dramatic.

15. The General Wolfe Approach. Back in 1759, General Wolfe defeated General Montcalm at Fortress Quebec by tricking the French commander into leaving the city to engage the British on the Plains of Abraham. Montcalm was defeated whereas he would have been able to defend himself behind the city walls. This is the strategy of inducing your opponent to leave the fortress and come to you. In this way you select the ground and thus, the rules of the engagement.

16. The Strategy of Patience. Do not press your opponents vigorously. A cornered enemy is extremely dangerous. Pursue with patience. Keep your opposition under observation. Keep your opposition on the run. When their energy has expired—move in for the capture.

17. Trading Glass for Diamonds. Offer something of apparent worth to motivate the production of something of more value. You need nectar to attract bees. You need money to attract money. You need power to attract power. Always project a greater wealth and power than you actually possess.

18. Capture the General to Subdue the Army. When your opposition is overwhelming, concentrate on taking out the leader.

19. Pouring Water on the Powder. If your opponent is powerful and cannot be defeated in a direct confrontation, you must concentrate on destroying resources and hurting the morale of the supporters of your opponent.

20. The Strategy of Confusion. Use confusion to your advantage. Take advantage of confusion among your opposition. Recruit support from amongst the ranks of your opposition by inciting confusion.

21. The Lobster Strategy. When a lobster sheds its shell, it leaves the appearance of being, while the living lobster has moved on. Sometimes a strategist must retain the facade of being in one place after having moved on to another place.

22. Lock the Hen House to Keep the Eggs. In other words, keep infiltrators from your opposition in check. If discovered, pretend that they have been undiscovered. Keep them under observation. If they escape, do not waste energy in pursuit.

23. Keep Your Allies Distant, Your Enemies Near. Never let your allies become familiar with your strength or weakness. Keep your relationship with your allies friendly but formal. Secrecy is your best shield for defense and your best sword for offense. Keep an eye on the movements of your allies. Watch your enemies very carefully and be aware of all their movements. Know your enemy intimately and your allies formally.

24. The Strategy of Manipulation. If you have two enemies and one is the enemy of the other, use the facilities of one enemy to defeat the mutual enemy of you and your gullible ally. After defeating the first enemy, turn the facilities of your "ally" to your advantage in defeating your second enemy on their own territory.

25. Seducing Your Opponent's Followers. Constantly seek to recruit talented followers of your opponent. This strengthens yourself and weakens your enemy.

26. The Art of Indirect Chastisement. If you need to criticize a valued soldier or ally, then criticize an inferior for the same offense and ensure that the valued party bears witness to the scolding.

27. The Strategy of Ignorance. To achieve an objective you may have to feign ignorance, stupidity or incompetence. But you must do so brilliantly. Your performance must not be obvious nor of such a nature that your strategy is betrayed.

28. The Point of No Return. You should manipulate your opposition into a position of no return by enticement with advantages and opportunities.

29. The Fireworks Strategy. If you can't achieve your aims through facts, then baffle your opposition with bullshit. Deceive with dazzling dramatics, fabricate fantasies fired forth with flair and shower your targets with flamboyance and fiery rhetoric. Give the public a circus and contain your message within. Educate through the media of entertainment. Exploit existing myths and create your own myths and legends.

30. The Transformation of Guest Into Host. Sometimes an organization can be taken over by a client. Beware of granting influence to a client, director or interested participating party within your organization. Watch your field agents closely for an indication of a desire for control and influence.

31. The Strategy of Feminine Beauty. This is the strategy that allows women to exploit the weakness in some men to be influenced by beauty and sexuality. Women can be more successful in many situations than a man, simply by using seduction as a strategy. In Africa in 1978, we were able to meet with a government Minister because we had a beautiful woman with our team. He told her anything we wanted to know. This is a strategy that will most certainly be criticized by eco-feminists but in doing so they sacrifice what is probably their most powerful approach to strategy. The feminine is a force that must be taken advantage of and this force includes the seduction of attraction and the appeal of sexual promise. At the same time, male Earth Warriors must be on the alert for this strategy being utilized against them. As an example, the Greenpeace office in New Zealand was successfully infiltrated by a French secret service agent who had some of the males there literally whispering confidential information into her ear. For the female Earth Warrior, all opportunities to gain advantage over male adversaries should be exploited. This strategy can also work for straight or gay men or women seeking to influence a gay man or woman. It is strategically advantageous to always take advantage of any weakness for the benefit of the cause or objective.

32. The Strategy of Vulnerability. When you appear weaker than you are, your opposition may make three mistakes. They may become conceited and complacent, giving you an advantage. They may become arrogant and aggressive, which will enable you to control their destruction. Or they may assume that you are attempting to trap them, which will motivate their retreat.

33. The Strategy of Double Agents. Attempt to compromise agents of your opposition so that they will be forced to work towards your advantage.

34. The Art of Being a Victim. Pretend to be a victim of your own organization so that you might win the confidence and support of your opposition.

35. The Strategy of Orbiting Circles. Never utilize just one strategy.

Always use numerous strategies. Change your tactics, innovate new tactics, give your imagination full rein, keep your opposition constantly on the move.

36. The Art of Retreat. When facing superior odds, you must never fight. You have three options. Surrender, compromise or flight. Surrender is complete defeat and is ill advised. Compromise means to be partially defeated and is a last resort. Flight means that you are not defeated. As long as you are not defeated, you have a chance to recover your strength and triumph.

Every problem has three solutions. You accept, you ignore or you resolve. To accept is unacceptable. To ignore is unacceptable. The only solution for an Earth Warrior is to resolve the problem. If a solution is not available then retreat from the situation until a solution can be found.

AFTER WORDS

In presenting this book on strategy, I have attempted to construct a foundation for the individual warrior.

The wisdom of Sun Tzu is meant to guide you. The strategy that needs to be developed for your individual needs and objectives must originate from within your intuitive soul and from no one else. Your intuitive strategy must be tempered by the fires of your own imagination and driven by the strength and power of your will.

Remember, always, that the strength of your will, the flames of your imagination, and the spirit of your intuition cannot triumph over the physical laws of the universe.

For every action there is an equal and opposite reaction. Thus the karmic laws must be respected.

Once the law of karma is understood, it becomes safe to move onto the next step of obtaining freedom.

Shadows can only pretend to be warriors. Shadows may go through the motions of a warrior, but they only mimic the true warrior. Humans who are enslaved to security, materialism, emotions, pleasure, pain, abuse, arrogance, appetite, and to dependence are only shadows.

We are locked into our suffering, and our pleasures are the seal. Only by utilizing the charts of imagination can we navigate our discipline to overcome the shadowy temptations of anthropocentric reality.

The first step to freedom is to transcend the anthropocentric reality. Place yourself spiritually beyond the reach of the pseudo-important myths of the self-centered human cultures. Once you have become spiritually armored, you can be free to mindfully participate with the folly of humanity.

A warrior is a being of power. Power can only be realized by discipline. Discipline can only be maintained by the will. The will must be fueled by the imagination. The imagination derives its power from the intuitive soul.

For your teachers, look to both the human and nonhuman peoples of the

Earth for your lessons. Learn by intuition to see wisdom and reject ignorance.

Above all, do not mire yourself in the muck of pettiness. All individual problems are resolvable, either by solution or by acceptance.

Do not concern yourself with what others might think of you. The strategy of an Earth warrior activist is to say unpopular things to piss people off, to undertake actions which anger and disturb people, and to boldly strike at issues and ideologies where none have dared to strike before.

> *"The only thing worse then being talked about,*
> *is not being talked about."*
> *- Oscar Wilde*

It is the duty of the Earth Warrior to use actions, voice, pen, and camera to provoke thoughts, and to motivate change. The warrior is a catalyst for change. The actions, objectives, and the exemplary life style of a warrior are more important then the mortal ego of the individual.

In choosing a warrior's way and dedicating my life to protecting and serving my planet, I have been richly rewarded.

Now, in my early forties, I can honestly say that I have been very much satisfied with my life and achievements. I have saved lives. Because I acted, hundreds of wolves and bison, thousands of whales and redwoods, tens of thousands of dolphins, and hundreds of thousands of seals have survived and have been given an opportunity to perpetuate more of their own kind.

If wolves, whales, dolphins, and redwoods survive the hominid holocaust, it will be in some small part because my crew and I had the audacity to intervene in the selfish affairs of anthropocentric humans.

> *"The man who is right is a majority. He who has God*
> *[Earth] and conscience on his side, has a majority.*
>
> *Though he does not represent the present state, he*
> *represents the future state. If he does not represent*
> *what we are, he represents what we ought to be."*
> *- Frederick Douglass,*
> *1818 - 1895*

Remember, always, that it is the nature of a warrior to act. Do not be daunted by the formidable strength of the opposition. Do not be depressed by doom and gloom predictions. A true warrior must welcome challenge and transform the impossible into the possible.

Because you live in these trying times, it is your task to confront situations created by human ignorance and apathy, and focus your actions through love for the future and all the children of all the children of all species.

Do not be embarrassed to howl with the wolves. Do not be afraid to swim with the sharks. Do not be so proud as to ignore the art of the spider, the wisdom of the whale, the strength of the ant, or the beauty of planet.

Above all, re-connect with the Earth. Feel the mud between your toes, smell the fragrance of the forests, dance with the stars, and exalt in your animalism.

Eat at the table of the Earthly mother. Drink when you are thirsty and eat when you are hungry. Squat when you shit and give nutrients to the forest floor when you are able to do so.

Sleep in the arms of the Earth with the stars above your head. Take every opportunity to do so.

Laugh when you are happy. Cry when you are sad. Scream forth your joy at the climax of sexual unification.

Be an animal, a primate, the outrageous monkey cousin that you are. Be alive and live, live, live.

The love of life inspires passion for life which motivates the passionate defense of life. And in a most ironic way, such passion for life allows the peaceful acceptance and understanding of the value your death has in the vibrant dance of the Continuum.

Environmental activists may be a nuisance and a pain in the ass to the established authorities of the present. However, to the establishment of the future, we will be honored ancestors.

—Captain Paul Watson

BIBLIOGRAPHY

Berry, Thomas *The Dream of Earth.*
Sierra Club Books. 1988.

Capra Fritjof
& Charlene Spretnak *Green Politics.*
E.P. Dutton. New York. 1984.

Catton, William *Overshoot—The Ecological Basis of
Revolutionary Change.*
University of Illinois Press. 1982.

Day, David *The Eco Wars.*
Key-Porter Books. Toronto. 1989.

Erenfeld, David *The Arrogance of Humanism.*
Oxford University Press. 1978.

Fields, Rick *The Code of the Warrior.*
Harper Perennial. New York. 1991.

Foreman, David *Ecodefense: A Field Guide to Monkeywrenching.*
Ned Ludd Books. Tucson, Arizona. 1985.

Hunter, Robert *Warriors of the Rainbow.*
Holt, Rinehart and Winston. New York. 1979.

Lovelock, J.E. *Gaia. A New Look at Life on Earth.*
Oxford University Press. 1979.

Machiavellii, Niccolo *Arte Della Guerra (The Art of War)*
Published in 1521.

Manes, Christopher. *Green Rage: Radical Environmentalism and the
Unmaking of Civilization.*
Little, Brown and Company. Boston. 1990.

McLuhan, Herbert Marshall
 The Mechanical Bride. 1951.
The Gutenburg Galaxy. 1964.
Understanding Media. 1964.
The Medium is the Massage. 1967.
The Laws of Media. 1988.
University of Toronto Press.

Musashi, Miyamoto	*A Book Of Five Rings.* A translation by Victor Harris. The Overlook Press. Woodstock, N.Y. 1974.
Nash, Roderick Frazier	*The Rights of Nature.* The University of Wisconsin Press. 1989.
Rolston III, Holmes	*Environmental Ethics.* Temple University Press. 1988.
Scarce, Rik	*Eco-Warriors—Understanding the Radical* *Environmental Movement.* Noble Press. Chicago. 1987.
Stone, Christopher.	*Earth and Other Ethics.* Harper & Row. New York. 1987.

Tzu, Sun.
   The following are the translations and interpretations used
   in the preparation of *Earthforce!*

Clavell, James	*The Art of War.* Delacourt Press, New York. 1983.
Cleary, Thomas	*The Art of War.* Shambhala Publications. Boston. 1988. *Mastering the Art of War.* A translation of Zhuge Liang's and Liu Ji's commentaries on the classic by Sun Tzu. Shambhala Publications. Boston. 1989.
Griffith, Samuel B.	*Sun Tzu. The Art of War.* Oxford University Press, Oxford. 1963.
Hanzhang, General Tao	*Sun Tzu's Art of War: The Modern Chinese* *Interpretation.* Translated by Yuan Shibing. Sterling Publishing. New York. 1987.
Wing, R.L.	*The Art Of Strategy: A New Translation of Sun* *Tzu's Classic The Art of War.* A Dolphin Book. Doubleday. New York. 1988.
Periodicals:	*Earth First! Journal* *Sea Shepherd Log* *Wild Earth*

115

INDEX

A
Abbey, Edward, (Quotes) 48, 67.
Allen, Woody (Quote) 48.
Alquonquin, 8.
Amchitka, protest at, 8.
Amiot, Father, 4.
Arizona Five, 39.
Arthur, King, 25.
B
Bardot, Brigitte, 87.
Berry, Father Thomas, 46.
Black Elk, Wallace, 8.
Bonaparte, Napoleon, 4-5.
Brower, David, 46.
Bush, George, 40.
C
Caldicott, Dr. Helen, 46.
Canadian Coast Guard, 9.
Catholic Church, 32.
Cormack, Captain John, 91.
Coronado, Rod, 78, 86.
D
Don't Make a Wave Committee, 9.
Douglass, Frederick, (Quote), 112.
E
Earth First!, 47, 59, 100.
Earth Island Institute, 46.
F
Federal Bureau of Investigation, (FBI), 100.
Friends of the Wolf, 85.
Foreman Dave, 47, 59, 61.
Fossey, Dian, (Quote) 62.
Fox, The, 103
G
Giap, General, 5.
Greenpeace, 9, 47, 73, 100, 104.
H
Hayduke, George Washington, (Quote) 93.
Hayes, Randy, 46.
Hood, Robin, 6.
Howitt, David, 78, 86.
Hunter, Robert, 47, 62.
Huron, 8.

I
Industrial Workers of the World, 106.
J
Jones, Captain John Paul, (Quotes) 60, 96.
K
Kennedy, John F., (Quote) 55.
Kirk, Captain James T., (Quote) 55.
Kohiro, Sasaki, 6.
L
LaBudde, Sam, 105.
Lakota, 8, 51.
Ling, King Wu, 4.
M
Mendes, Chico, 47.
Millett, Peg, (Quote) 70.
McLuhan, Corinne, 3.
McLuhan, Marshall, 2-4, 7, 10, 61,
(Quotes) 41, 43-44.
McTaggart, David, 104.
Morse-Brown, Sam, 3.
Montcalm, General, 106
Musashi, Miyamoto, 2-4, 6-7, 10, 103,
(Quotes) 44, 51.
N
North, Colonel Oliver, 92.
North Vietnamese Army, (NVA), 5.
O
Osaka Castle, seige of, 6.
P
Physicians for Nuclear Responsibility, 46.
Q
Quebec, Fortress of, 106.
R
Rainbow Warrior, 100.
Rainforest Action Network, 46.
Rainforest Information Center, 46.
Reagan, Ronald, 42, 92.
Roselle, Mike, 47.
S
Salish, 8.
Sea Shepherd Conservation Society, 9, 86.
Seattle, Chief, (Quote) 26.
Seed, John, 46.

Sekigahara, battle of, 6.
Shimbara, battle of, 6.
Shuson (Haiku) 59.
Sierra (whaling ship), 86, 100.
Simon Fraser University, 9.
Squamish Five, 39.
Sun Tzu, 2-5, 10, 111. (Quote) 73.
Supreme Court of Canada, 86.
T
Toronto, University of, 6.
V
Van Gogh, Vincent, 18.
Viet Cong, (VC), 5.
W
Watson, Paul, 3, 8, (Quote), 44.
Western Canada Wilderness Committee, 85.
Wild Earth Society, 47.
Wilde, Oscar (Quote), 112.
Wolfe, General James, 106.
Wounded Knee, 8.
Wu Ling, King, 4.
Y
Yoshioka, School of swordsmanship, 6.

The author invites both criticisms and suggestions. A second edition of this book will be published in 1994. This edition can be enhanced with contributions by Earth warriors who have both knowledge and experience with strategy in application to environmental and conservation issues.

Write to:

Captain Paul Watson
5218 Donna Maria Lane
La Cañada, California 91011
U.S.A.
Fax: 310-394-0360.